LANGUAGE AND CONTENT

BERNARD A. MOHAN
University of British Columbia

D1009986

ADDISON-WESLEY PUBLISHING COMPANY
Reading, Massachusetts
Menlo Park, California • New York • Don Mills, Ontario
Wokingham, England • Amsterdam • Sydney • Singapore
Tokyo • Mexico City • Bogotá • Santiago • San Juan

THE ADDISON-WESLEY SECOND LANGUAGE PROFESSIONAL LIBRARY SERIES

Sandra J. Savignon
Consulting Editor

HIGGINS, John and JOHNS, Tim
Computers in Language Learning

SMITH, Stephen M.
The Theater Arts and the Teaching of Second Languages

SAVIGNON, Sandra J.
Communicative Competence : Theory and Classroom Practice

VENTRIGLIA, Linda
Conversations of Miguel and Maria

SAVIGNON, Sandra J. and BERNS, Margie S.
Initiatives in Communicative Language Teaching

WALLERSTEIN, Nina
Language and Culture in Conflict

Acknowledgments
Pages 30–33, Courtesy of *The Westcoast Reader* and photographer, Josh Berson.

Library of Congress Cataloging in Publication Data

Mohan, Bernard A.
  Language and content.

  Includes bibliographies.
    1. Language and languages—Study and teaching.
2. Language and education. I. Title.
P51.M58   1985   418'.007   84-24311
ISBN 0-201-05288-1

ISBN 0-201-05288-1
CDEFGHIJKLM-MU-99876543210

Preface

While the need for coordinating the learning of language and subject matter is generally recognized, just how this should be accomplished remains a problem. This book is an exploration into some of the ways these two areas can be coordinated.

The importance of subject matter and content as a context for language learning is now generally acknowledged in second language research. Similarly, in first language education there has been much discussion of 'language across the curriculum' since the publication of the Bullock Report "A Language for Life" (Bullock Committee, 1975). As a result, it has become widely accepted that the teaching of language should be integrated with all aspects of the curriculum. "Learning, it is now clear, involves language not merely as a passive medium for receiving concepts. Thus learning is not merely through language but with language. The task of devising a policy adequate for this is now laid on every school." (Maryland, 1977, ix).

We cannot achieve this goal if we assume that language learning and subject-matter learning are totally separate and unrelated operations. Yet language and subject matter are still standardly considered in isolation from each other. And, in fact, historical trends toward greater specialization in schooling and in academic disciplines have, if anything, militated against an integrated perspective, both in practice and in theory.

It is clear that the task of devising a policy for the integration of language and subject areas calls for the development of a more integrated model of language and content learning than presently exists. And, in turn, this model needs to provide clear guidelines for educational policy as well as a theoretical background to educational policy.

The task of developing such a model is the main purpose of this book. In discussing the integration of language and content learning, the book addresses both classroom concerns and research concerns. Typically, each chapter begins with a classroom issue using simple examples, and later the chapter develops the theoretical implications of the issue. Consequently, readers with greater interest in classroom issues will find these in earlier parts of chapters, and readers concerned with research and theory will also be interested in later parts.

CLASSROOM ISSUES

If teachers are to integrate language and content in the classroom, they need ways of organizing material to aid both the development of language and the development of understanding. They also need ways of coordinating language objectives with content area objectives.

The strategies offered in this book pay particular attention to students who must learn through the medium of English as a second language. These students need to learn unfamiliar subject matter in an unfamiliar language. Language teachers must find ways to help these students learn the language needed to study subject matter in English, while content teachers must devise strategies to help such students understand content and become more independent learners. The joint task of both these groups of teachers is to provide for understandable communication, cumulative language learning, and the development of academic thinking skills.

A policy that promotes these goals is of value to all educators, since language is important in all aspects of education. The integration of language and subject areas is relevant to all teachers, whether they teach language or subject matter, and whether they teach second language learners or native speakers.

Nevertheless, many discussions of language learning and teaching continue to ignore content. Often the assumption is that the language teacher is solely concerned with language and the content teacher is solely concerned with content. This is clearly wrong. It needs to be recognized that content means not only the subject matter of the content class but also the topics which are discussed in the language class. Whenever the language teacher and students communicate, they communicate about something, about some topic or content. It is absurd to ignore the role of content in the language class, just as it is absurd to ignore the role of language as a medium of learning in the content class. Every language teacher has to organize content material to support language learning, and all language teachers have an interest in doing this more systematically.

My approach starts from the fact that all teachers must communicate about content with their students. Beginning with the teaching of topics, I outline a systematic framework for relating language and content that applies across the curriculum. Using classroom examples, it brings together issues which are often left separated: how we communicate knowledge through both language and graphics; how tests can confuse language requirements and content requirements. While the examples used for illustration are necessarily specific to particular groups of learners, I have found that even inexperienced teachers can generalize from the examples and apply the approach to their own teaching situation.

While I do concentrate on specific classroom examples and strategies, the approach is not limited to classroom contexts. Based as it is on the activities of society, it naturally extends to learning in the community. Nor does the approach assume that there must be a conflict between language teaching and informal language acquisition. Rather, it takes the view that one aim of education is to relate formal and informal learning so that the one builds upon the other. This is fundamental to an educational policy of active concern for the language and educational development of learners in classrooms and community.

THEORY AND RESEARCH

Of course, classroom strategies and approaches require a theoretical framework. Language and content must be related theoretically.

Current views of language teaching can be broadly termed "communicative." Communicative or functional language teaching derives from a functional or contextual view of language which relates discourse to extralinguistic context or situation (as contrasted with a formal view of language as an abstract system). Research in the 1970s gave much attention to the functions of language and to speech acts such as requests. This led to the question of how hearers recognize an utterance as having a function (for instance, how contextual understandings enable us to interpret an utterance as a request). In consequence, there is now an increased interest in the notion of speech events, that is, culturally recognized social activities in which language plays a role (such as religious services or parliamentary debates). These activities are sets of contextual understandings. They are "life-worlds" of everyday knowledge. They provide schemata, frames, or bodies of everyday knowledge that give an inferential base for the understanding of utterances (see Levinson, 1983:279–283).

But the contextual view of language lacks an adequate model of contexts: while a contextual view of language relies on activities as contexts for discourse, we do not have a general model of activities and of their relation to discourse. Therefore, my primary aim in developing a "knowledge framework" for activities was to describe what such a model could look like. In pursuing the model, it was necessary to tackle issues of central concern to pragmatics and sociolinguistics.

1) What is the role of nonlinguistic knowledge in the interpretation of discourse?

It is obvious that nonlinguistic knowledge influences the interpretation of discourse. This is well accepted and amply proven. What we now need to explore are the relative roles of linguistic and nonlinguistic inference in the interpretation of different types of discourse.

Linguistic and non-linguistic inference are illuminated rather clearly in testing and evaluation. Many tests require students to make inferences from statements in test items. Achievement tests are specifically designed to distinguish between students who possess a given body of knowledge and those who do not. Thus achievement tests provide many demonstrations that non-linguistic knowledge affects the interpretation of discourse. Since inference in test items also draws on linguistic knowledge, an examination of the ways in which tests confuse requirements for knowledge of language and knowledge of content can lead to a better understanding of the relative roles of linguistic and non-linguistic inference.

2) How are activities learned, and what role does discourse play in this process?

Just as it is obvious that context adds meanings to discourse, it is equally obvious that discourse adds meanings to context. But do these two processes conflict? Or are they mutually supportive, and if so, how?

In the tradition of Dewey, education can be defined as the initiation of the learner into the activities of society. The central role of discourse in education then is to develop the learner's understanding of an activity. In this view discourse adds to the body of non-linguistic knowledge of an activity. Compare this to the previous question. There evaluation tested knowledge; here education develops knowledge. This contrast is similar to the distinction between context-dependent and context-independent discourse. But educational discourse is not absolutely context-independent discourse. The case of students who must learn through the medium of a second language shows there must be a complex interplay between context-dependence and context-independence in educational discourse. Since such students have difficulty with the language of instruction, they cannot learn solely through language. In this book I explore this interplay in educational discourse.

3) Do activities have a common pattern or framework?

As we have said, the contextual view of language lacks a general model of activities. We need a general model, because without it the concept of an activity is too vague and we cannot generalize from one activity to another.

This book outlines just such a general model. It argues that there is a general framework for the body of knowledge in an activity. An activity is a mode of thought and conduct. An activity has a pattern of action which includes description, sequence, and choice, and involves background knowledge which includes classification, principles, and evaluation. This claim is illustrated by everyday examples and is based on the logical analysis of these structures of knowledge. It forms a unified picture from a wide range of different research literatures. Classification, choice or decision making and the other elements have a diverse literature which establishes them as categories of knowledge and as thinking processes.

4) How do activities relate to discourse?

One way activities relate to discourse is that an activity provides contextual understandings which help us to interpret utterances: this relation between activity and discourse is prominent in the literature of pragmatics. But there are a number of other relations which need to be explored. Once we have a general model for activities, we can see other possibilities.

In action dialogues knowledge about an activity is usually implicit. In expository discourse it is made explicit. The most direct reflection of the framework of an activity can be seen in discourses that make knowledge of an activity explicit: discourses that provide descriptions, narrate sequences, elaborate decision situations, and state classifications, principles, and evaluations. The framework accounts for these discourse types and provides a reworking of traditional rhetorical categories such as description, narration, and argument. Within an activity all of these kinds of discourse are possible, and the concept of an activity enables us to see the connections between them more clearly.

The concept of an activity, then, when carefully defined, provides a framework which relates language and content. The central purpose of this book is to communicate a broad sense of how this works in practice and in theory. It would not be possible in this book to develop the ideas in full detail or to refer to all of the relevant literature, and I have not attempted to do so. My aim is rather to outline a perspective which coordinates diverse sources of theory and practice and to illustrate it through everyday examples.

THE PLAN OF THIS BOOK

Chapter 1 discusses the case of students who must learn through the medium of English as a second language and relates this to the larger question of language across the curriculum. It points to the need for a framework that integrates language and content. Chapter 2 illustrates the required framework through the task of teaching a theme or topic. It then generalizes this framework by connecting it with the concept of an activity. Chapter 3 analyzes the action situations of an activity as structures of description, sequence, and choice, illustrates ways of representing these structures, and discusses the place of action dialogues and the language of description, sequence, and choice. Chapter 4 analyzes the background knowledge of an activity as structures of classification, principles, and evaluation, illustrates the representation of these structures, and indicates ways they are expressed in language. Chapter 5 deals with the issue of sequencing learning from specific action situations to general background knowledge. Discourse in action situations is typically highly context-dependent practical discourse; general background knowledge is typically associated with relatively context-independent theoretical discourse. Chapter 6 shows how the relation of language and content raises important questions in testing and evaluation. Noting ways in which test items can be biased against second language learners from another culture, it draws attention to the content component in language tests and the language component in tests of achievement in content areas.

ACKNOWLEDGMENTS

Preliminary versions of some of the ideas presented here have appeared in some of my articles, and I wish to thank TESOL and the Ontario Ministry of Culture and Recreation for permission to quote from this material. In addition, I am grateful to the editorial advisory board of the *Westcoast Reader*, the photographer, Josh Berson, and to the Insurance Corporation of British Columbia for use of the example material in Chapter 2.

The preparation of this book drew on the help and encouragement of many people. Margaret Early, Carol Thew, and Patricia Wakefield have taken the model developed in this book and implemented it in a resource book for teaching English as a second language across the curriculum. Their sustained input and feedback deserves special thanks. Meryl Arnott, Lee Coulter, Naomi Katz, and Helen Vanwel have taken aspects of the model and developed classroom materials for them. Various other colleagues in Canada, the United States, and Britain gave their time to read parts of the manuscript or talk through various ideas. My thanks to Chris Brumfit, Ron Cowan, Mike Long, Sandra Savignon, Merrill Swain, Norman Whitney, and Henry Widdowson. And Phyllis Mitzman, my editor at Addison-Wesley, had the unenviable task of untangling many a sentence. Finally a word of appreciation to my wife, Marilyn, who listened to many of my ideas and found out more about language and content than she could possibly want to know.

Although I believe the ideas in this book have applicability across all language and content areas, the examples are drawn from English as a second language. My concluding thanks therefore to ESL teachers and researchers for creating an enthusiastic and supportive environment for encouraging and pursuing new ideas.

Bernard A. Mohan

Contents

Chapter 1

Language as a Medium of Learning

1.1 INTRODUCTION

Throughout the world millions of people receive education and training in a language which is not their mother tongue: Hispanic students in the United States, immigrant students in Canada and Europe, secondary school students in Nigeria and other African countries, university students studying abroad, employees in training at numerous international corporations. In many cases these learners fail to reach their potential in academic achievement because their language learning is poorly coordinated with their learning of content or subject matter.

Any educational approach that considers language learning alone and ignores the learning of subject matter is inadequate to the needs of these learners. Yet much educational thinking treats language learning and content learning separately. And this is surprising, since education is fundamentally a process which occurs through the use of language. Language is the major medium of instruction and learning.

The case of these learners points to an issue at the heart of language education and research. A language is a system that relates what is being talked about (content) and the means used to talk about it (expression). Linguistic content is inseparable from linguistic expression. But in research and in classroom practice, this relationship is frequently ignored. In subject matter learning we overlook the role of language as a medium of learning. In language learning we overlook the fact that content is being communicated.

This is not to imply that language is the sole medium of learning, for the learner also acquires knowledge contextually while participating in shared activities in a social setting. This is most clearly seen when we recognize that education is not limited to formal instruction, but also occurs by socialization and enculturation throughout society. What is needed is a integrative approach which relates language learning and content learning, considers language as a medium of learning, and acknowledges the role of context in communication. Such an approach will not only be of value for students

1

learning through a second language, it will have implications for all language learners. And it will have implications for education in general.

From language in isolation to language as a medium of learning

The contrast between language taught for its own sake and language as a medium of learning is a familiar one to language teachers. We see language taught for its own sake in James Joyce's *Portrait of the Artist as a Young Man*. There, in the passage that deals with the Latin lesson, Joyce shows the teacher holding language at a distance and manipulating it. His main interest is its form and correctness as an index of scholastic virtue, and all shortcomings are roundly condemned.

> Father Arnall came in and the Latin lesson began and he remained still, leaning on the desk with his arms folded. Father Arnall gave out the theme-books and he said that they were scandalous and that they were all to be written out again with the corrections at once. But the worst of all was Fleming's theme because the pages were stuck together by a blot: and Father Arnall held it up by a corner and said it was an insult to any master to send him up such a theme. Then he asked Jack Lawton to decline the noun *mare* and Jack Lawton stopped at the ablative singular and could not go on with the plural.
>
> "You should be ashamed of yourself," said Father Arnall sternly. "You, the leader of the class!"
>
> Then he asked the next boy and the next and the next. Nobody knew. Father Arnall became very quiet, more and more quiet as each boy tried to answer it and could not.

Fortunately, there has been significant progress in language teaching since Joyce's time. A major feature of recent work has been the attention given to language as a medium of learning, to language in use, to language playing a role in education, work, and social interaction. This has not been limited to one area of language education: it can be seen in first language teaching, in second language teaching, in teaching children as well as adults, in teaching those with academic and those with occupational goals. We find this modern emphasis on language as a medium of learning in the work of many North American and British writers.

Cazden, in discussing first language teaching with children, says:

> We must always remember that language is learned, not because we want to talk or read or write about language, but because we want to talk and read and write about the world. Only linguists have language as their subject matter. For the rest of us—especially for children—language is the medium of interpersonal relationships, the medium of our mental life, the medium of learning about the world (Cazden, 1977:42).

MacFarlane, dealing with adult literacy, is guided by similar principles:

The book is written in the belief that the best way to become an effective reader and writer is to learn by starting with the *uses* the learner wishes to make of literacy. Only in that setting will the 'how' of those uses make real sense (MacFarlane, 1979:V).

And, Tucker and D'Angeljan view second language in the same way.

The student can most effectively acquire a second language when the task of language learning becomes incidental to the task of communicating with someone... about some topic . . . which is inherently interesting to the student (Tucker and D'Anglejan, 1975:162).

Language is normally a medium of learning about the world. A child communicating with a mother is learning about the world, and learns language in the process of learning about the world. Both in research and in classroom practice it makes little sense to disconnect language learning from learning about the world. There is no reason for research to be restricted to the study of language learning in isolation from content learning and from contexts of communication. There is no reason for the language classroom to be restricted to teaching language for its own sake. Even in the traditional Latin class, students often learned about Roman civilization, and learned Latin in the process of doing so. Language as a medium of learning is of importance to every language teacher, and indeed to every teacher.

Although this book will deal mainly with language as a medium of learning in second language work, the principles apply to the whole field of language education.

1.2 LANGUAGE AS A MEDIUM OF LEARNING IN ESL TEACHING

Anyone coming into an English language environment from a different language background will have some problems adapting. However, ESL students with little or no English, who must suddenly attend schools where English is the language of instruction, provide an extreme example of the issues that arise when the second language is a medium of learning. ESL students need to acquire English, as well as learn difficult subject matter through English. There may have been little continuity in their educational experiences in their home country, yet at the end of their secondary education, their level of academic achievement in English and their level of subject matter knowledge will be judged by comparison with English-speaking students.

While this may seem to be a hopeless situation, it is in the very schools these students attend that the resources exist for investigating possible solutions to the problem. Teachers of English as a second language, teachers of English as a first language, and teachers of different subject areas work in the same institution in everyday contact. Information on what is taught and how it is taught is publicly available, and curricula and textbooks are accessible. Most importantly, there is concern for the role of language and learning across the whole curriculum and interest in putting this concern into practice.

There have been three stages in the recent development of educational policy for ESL learners:

1. *Learning by exposure to an English-speaking community.* The learner is left to pick up English through informal language learning.

2. *Isolated language teaching.* The learner is engaged in formal language learning by direct language teaching as a separate and isolated activity.

3. *Interactive language teaching—language teaching for and through the normal activities of the school and the English-speaking community; language teaching through content and for content.* Positive steps are taken to improve informal language learning in the community. Positive steps are taken to relate the language course to the communicative environment. Interactive language teaching is an educational policy which recognizes the importance of language as a medium of learning.

One ever-present question in language learning research is whether informal language learning is more effective than formal language learning. It is frequently assumed that there are only these two alternatives. The more relevant question is how to develop interactive teaching—the third alternative. In fact, industrial language training already provides an example of interactive teaching: it explores the communicative environment and relates the language course to this environment.

Interactive language teaching: the example of industrial language training

Industrial language training is a good example of interactive teaching where positive steps have been taken to relate the language course to the communicative environment. For immigrants, one communicative environment is their workplace.

Immigrants in work situations not only need to understand job-related language, they also need to communicate socially both inside and outside of work. An organization that deals with this group is the British National Centre for Industrial Language Training, which began by providing language training for Asian employees at their places of employment. (See Jupp and Hodlin, 1975, Laird, 1977, Gubbay, 1978).

Establishing and running a training course in the workplace has three main stages: investigation of the workplace, course planning, and operating the course. Investigation of the workplace includes discussions with management (issues relating to immigrant workers), with the union (problems immigrant workers have in understanding and participating in the union), touring the factory to understand the work processes, collecting job descriptions, and pinpointing the nature of specific problems. Course planning then covers working out the communications network of the students selected for the course (who do they normally communicate with?), describing their daily timetable and the situations in which they use English, understanding the broad language functions which are usual within their roles, and identifying their linguistic, informational and behavioral/cultural communicative needs. For instance, hospital workers may need knowledge of special hazards, to be aware of their responsibility for safety, as well as to give warnings in English. Then a course syllabus is assembled that includes this information. Finally, operating the course is seen as a strategy of intervention in the work communication environment.

Communicative work transactions are frequently recorded, or role played, with supervisors and workers playing their work roles, and analyzed inductively with the students. To take an example of an actual exchange:

Operative: Excuse me.
Supervisor: Yes, Mrs. B.
Operative: I want the day off tomorrow.

In class, the discussion may show that the operative has blurted out the request without sufficient preparation. Leading phrases such as *Can I see you for a minute?* or explanations for the very short notice could be introduced. The importance of such phrases is that they will help employees succeed in short term aims (getting the day off) as well as the long term aim of maintaining a good working relationship with supervisors. This is much more than a matter of learning politeness expressions in English. Clearly the aim here goes beyond language training to the development of human relations communications skills.

In general, Jupp and Hodlin (*Industrial English*, 1975) see the immigrant in the work situation as climbing a 'language ladder' running from general isolation and understanding only simple language, to having enough work language to be fully flexible and pick up a new job. A major aim of the course is then to create the conditions for learning to persist after the course and for the learner to move up the ladder.

In fact, the work situation is seen as a language and communication learning environment having a mix of favorable and unfavorable situations. One aim of the course is to overcome some of the unfavorable situations. While work may provide opportunities to interact with native speakers, there may also be concentrations of non-native speakers on certain shifts, the noise level may be high, there may be cultural and other inhibitions on the part both of the immigrant and native personnel, and there may be difficult and stressful situations leading to conflict and communication breakdown between worker and supervisor, not to mention accidents and injuries. However, it should not be thought that the sole aim of the course is to make employees more effective workers. Language for social relations is an immediate priority; a broader aim is to equip immigrants to live in the host country by means of their learning and adjustment at the place of work.

Contrast this example of interactive language learning with the more traditional in-class, language centered general course that follows a grammar syllabus aimed at

a general competence in the language. In interactive language teaching, the ESL
teacher would:

1. *Analyze the learners' needs.* Often the traditional language course assumes that
   whatever is taught in the course is needed by the learner. Analyzing the learners'
   needs, goals and problems typically means interviewing both learners and
   those who work and interact with them to find out about the learners' present
   and future roles.

2. *Describe the learners' communicative environment outside of the language class.*
   The traditional language course usually ignores this. Describing the communicative environment can require: observing the learner outside of class, finding
   out the learners' daily or weekly pattern, interviewing the learners about their
   communication situation.

3. *Relate class activities to the learners' communication needs.* The traditional
   language class teaches language items and language skills. It may have little
   relevance to the learners' needs. By contrast, the way *Industrial English* uses
   communicative work transactions in class does make a connection with the
   learners' problems. Making this connection means looking at the learners'
   communication tasks to see how the language teacher can help, and developing
   suitable activities and materials.

4. *Find frameworks which make a bridge between language items and skills on the
   one hand, and learners' communication needs on the other.* Commenting on their
   course syllabus, Jupp and Hodlin say: "The overall scheme of subject matter
   and language content aims to bring together a number of factors such as language
   code, role, situation and message" (ibid: 50). The traditional course does not do
   this, being mainly concerned with teaching the language code. Useful bridging
   frameworks are centers of organization such as communicative work transactions, language functions (e.g., requests), and lists of study skills. Frameworks
   are important both for course planning and for assembling information about
   communication needs.

1.3 LANGUAGE ACROSS
THE CURRICULUM

The content class as a
communicative environment of
the learner

The communicative environment of workers is the workplace. But for students, the
communicative environment is the school or university, and in particular their content
classes of mathematics, social studies, and so on. These are the classes they attend in
addition to the language class. Many of the questions related to industrial language
training must also be asked of the academic setting. What are the communication

problems of the students? What are the content teacher's views of these problems, and who should take responsibility for working towards a solution? What is the mix of favorable and unfavorable situations in the content classes as communication learning environments? What sort of close, problem-centered interaction is possible between language assistance and the demands of the content class? What sort of organizational pattern is useful for relating language work to content classes?

In the more traditional view that regards language in isolation, the language teacher's concern was with language only, and the chemistry teacher's concern was with chemistry. It was supposed that there was no overlap and no demarcation problem. The traditional view, naturally enough, looked at language classes from the viewpoint of the language teacher, and looked at content classes from the viewpoint of the content teacher. But to look at the communicative environment of learners in the school, we must ask what is the relationship between language classes and content classes.

This means that we must look at language and learning across the whole curriculum: language and learning in the content class, as well as language and learning in the language class. We need an organizing framework for investigating and planning language and learning across the curriculum. At present, no adequate framework exists, but we can look at the work of researchers and practitioners concerned with language across the curriculum to see what the research suggests a framework should include.

*Language and learning in the
content class*

Recent research on language and learning in the content class suggests that we need more than a laissez-faire approach to help students with the language demands of the content class. A central concern of research conducted on second language acquisition is the extent to which second language learners are able to learn the second language in the content classroom, and this research contradicts the older laissez-faire arguments.

Laissez-faire supporters argue that second language students can learn English simply by exposure to schooling in an English-speaking community. Some can. Some students can learn to speak English, acquire the academic skills of reading and writing in a second language, reach their potential in academic achievement, and manage the necessary social, emotional, and cultural adjustments. Others cannot.

Rhode Island State Representative John Assalone, whose Italian immigrant father was thrown down the steps of a New York school for not speaking English, has said, "Immigrants should learn English like my father did, without burdening the American taxpayer to support expensive and failing programs" (*Newsweek*, 1980:93).

Salvatore Luciano entered New York schools at the age of nine and learned English the way Mr. Assalone's father did. In Salvatore's own words:

All the other kids in my class was like little babies but they could talk English and I didn't know what the —— they was sayin'. Maybe that's why I fought so hard to

get outta school, out into the streets where a lotta people spoke Sicilian-Italian and
they knew what I was sayin' and I could understand them. I picked up my English
on the streets. That's one thing I regret more than anything else, that my grammar is
lousy and I dont't have too many good words and I talk with a New York accent
(Gosch and Hammer, 1974:13).
Salvatore graduated to the Mafia, later becoming known to the world as Lucky Luciano.

Students learning English by exposure can pay considerable human costs. The
school has a responsibility to these students as it has to all students. Exposure to schooling
in English is an important resource in second language learning, but it is a resource
which has to be actively developed by teachers and administrators.

Those who claim that the best method for learning a second language is simply
to use it, generally see formal language teaching as grammatical explanations and drills.
If this recommendation means simply that the language teacher should spend more
time getting the students to talk and to take advantage of native speakers and other
second language use in their environment, few would disagree. But what about the
much more radical idea of abandoning formal language courses altogether and replacing
them with content courses in the second language? This gets rid of the grammar and
drills, provides an undoubted source of real language use and teaches the learners
valuable information or skills. Abandoning formal language classes is recommended
by two very different types of people: those who are thinking of eliminating the expense
of language classes (why can't they just pick up the language?) and those who are thinking
of the learner's capacities for first and second language acquisition and want to adopt a
laissez-faire position (why should the language teacher 'interfere' with or 'intervene in'
the course of language development?).

It might appear, at first, that rigorous research supports the laissez-faire approach.
Consider the research on French immersion programs, where a range of school subjects
are taught through French. These programs lead to a level of achievement in French
higher than that of students following courses in French as a second language (Swain,
1974). Similar results were obtained from an adult college ESL program by Mason
(1971). He compared foreign students taking an intensive ESL course with a matched
group following regular academic programs and found no significant differences in
achievement in English skills. Generalizing from these results it is easy to reach striking
conclusions about courses that attempt to teach a second language directly: they should
be replaced by content courses in the target language; all second language students
should simply be placed in such content courses; language curriculum planning is
irrelevant and redundant.

In fact, the research evidence on this point is contradictory. The experience of
Hispanic students immersed in English-language schools in the U.S.A. has proved to
be far less successful than the French immersion results in Canada (Cohen and Swain,
1976). Cummins (1979), reviewing the research literature, pointed out that immersion
programs for the majority language child result in high levels of functional bilingualism
and academic achievement; yet for many minority language children they lead to

inadequate command of both first and second languages and poor academic achievement. Fillmore (1982) indicated large individual differences between second language learners, finding that up to 25% of these learners had acquired very little English after three years of exposure to English in school and were in need of a long period of special instruction to prepare them to function effectively in an English-speaking classroom. Long (1983) reviewed the research on the question, Does second language instruction promote second language acquisition? He found some studies concluded that instruction does not help, while other studies found it beneficial. When Long did a careful reanalysis of the studies, he concluded that there is considerable evidence that second language instruction is beneficial.

How then can content teaching help language learning? A widely accepted explanation is that content teaching puts the emphasis on communicating information, not on the language used: "The student can most effectively acquire a second language when the task of language learning becomes incidental to the task of communicating with someone . . . about some topic . . . which is inherently interesting to the student" (Tucker and D'Anglejan, 1975).

As part of his theory of second language acquisition, Krashen (1982) states his 'input hypothesis': language acquisition occurs when the acquirer *understands* input language. This fits common sense. A person who wanted to learn Russian and also wanted to learn nuclear physics would not choose to attend a course in nuclear physics taught in Russian. The likely result would be to learn neither. The content teaching strategy will not work if the learners do not understand the discourse of the content course. They need some grasp of what is happening, even if it is not perfect. How, then, do you pick the right content courses? What makes them good or bad language environments? Here practice seems to be ahead of research and theory.

Many schools have moved away from the practice of inserting a new immigrant student into all school classes. There is now a more selective policy. Stoddart and Stoddart, writing about the British situation, feel that while children in the first grade can learn English solely through their regular classes (particularly when they work with class groups on practical projects), it becomes more difficult at the higher grade levels. At these higher levels certain subjects are more favorable than others for learning a second language through content: physical education, art and craft subjects, for example. What seems to them to distinguish the earlier grades from the later ones and favorable from unfavorable subjects, is practical activity. These are content classes "in which language is regularly used in connection with certain visible situations which illustrate its meaning" (Stoddart and Stoddart, 1968:63). A second important factor is whether the content is familiar to the student, i.e., whether he has studied the subject in his home country.

The selective policy is thus based on the possibility of language use in content classrooms being helped by visible situations or familiar situations. That is, it is an application to content teaching of the language teaching principle that "language teaching must be situational" (Billows, 1961:6). It tries to avoid placing students in a position where they learn neither language nor content. Rather, it aims to assign them to a successfully communicative classroom, where the students can comprehend the material and the teacher's messages, and the teacher can comprehend the students' messages sufficiently for feedback.

It appears, therefore, that content teaching has a great deal to offer, and we should use the opportunities it provides. Experience with situational content classes seems sufficiently successful that the selective placement policy should continue.

But at the same time, it should be remembered that it is not sufficient to look at content teaching solely as a means of language learning. A school in the United States could operate a policy of selective placement in content classes and have a staff of content teachers who were prepared to take responsibility for working for comprehension with second language learners and still be in violation of the law with respect to the educational interests of these students. The courts have decreed that it is discriminatory for the schools as public agencies not to make special provision for students from non-English speaking backgrounds. This is because, in the absence of special provision, these students are denied a meaningful opportunity to participate in the public educational program.

> Under these state-imposed standards [of requiring that English shall be the basic language of instruction in all schools and of requiring a standard of proficiency in English for graduation] there is no equality of treatment merely by providing students with the same facilities, textbooks, teachers and curriculum; for students who do not understand English are effectively foreclosed from any meaningful education. Basic English skills are at the very core of what these public schools teach. Imposition of a requirement that, before a child can affectively participate in the educational program, he must already have acquired those basic skills is to make a mockery of public education. We know that those who do not understand English are certain to find their classroom experiences wholly incomprehensible and in no way meaningful (Lau vs. Nichols, Supreme Court of the U.S., in Saville-Troike, 1976:146).

The main point here is not that it is discriminatory to require English for graduation without providing special instruction in it, but that with English as the medium of instruction these students are being denied the full benefit of the education offered, and therefore the school system must take affirmative steps to rectify this situation. It is all very well to use the math class as a resource for learning English, but the students' interests in gaining an education in mathematics cannot be neglected. Unlike deficiencies in other subjects, a deficiency in the language of instruction is a fundamental obstacle to education in all subjects.

In brief, second language learners need more than a laissez-faire approach. To be successful, content classes in the second language should be essentially understandable to the second language student. Language in the content class should be the target of an active policy across the curriculum, but it should not be assumed that it is easy to achieve this goal.

We have seen that it is a mistake to regard second language learning as the sole issue. Second language students cannot be denied the full benefit of the education offered; they must learn the subject matter of content classes also. A laissez-faire, sink-or-swim position, or one which considers these students solely as language learners is a violation of their right to an education. This means that we must go beyond second language acquisition research and consider the cognitive and academic language skills needed to study school subjects in English.

Writing and reading in the
content class

The selective placement policy is a strategy for placing second language learners into content classes to assist the students' language learning and content learning. It is a strategy for second language learners across the curriculum. Two groups have examined other strategies for language and learning in the content class: those who are concerned with writing across the curriculum (abbreviated to WATC here) and those who are concerned with reading in the content areas (abbreviated to RICA here). Both WATC and RICA examine first language learning, across the curriculum. Their strategies have implications for second language students in the content classroom since content classes require academic reading and writing of all students. After all, strategies which have proved to be necessary for first language learners are likely to be even more crucial for second language learners.

WRITING ACROSS
THE CURRICULUM

In 1975 a committee of inquiry into language in British schools published its findings in the Bullock Report, a main recommendation of which was that there should be "an organised policy for language across the curriculum in every school, establishing every teacher's involvement in language and reading development." Following this recommendation, Martin et al., (1976) give a detailed account of writing across the curriculum (WATC). The WATC approach was initially a theory of advanced first language acquisition—an early report was titled "The Development of Writing Abilities, 11–18"—and the research project was concerned with the way writing ability develops. In the WATC view, the three central functions of writing are the expressive, the transactional, and the poetic. The expressive is basic. It is "the means by which the new is tentatively explored, thoughts may be half-uttered"; it is crucial for "trying out and coming to terms with new ideas. Because it is the kind of writing in which we most fully reveal ourselves to our reader—in a trusting relationship—it is instrumental in setting up a dialogue between writer and reader from which both can learn." It is central for learning to write, "the seed bed from which more specialised and differentiated kinds of writing can grow—towards the greater explicitness of the transactional or the more conscious shaping of the poetic."

However, in their large survey of writing across the content areas by 11–18 year olds, the team found secondary school writing to be mainly in the transactional function, written for the teacher as examiner. This they viewed negatively, believing that the demand for impersonal inexpressive writing can inhibit learning. They noted the lack of opportunity for the expressive to play its role in learning to write. Consequently their recommendation was for the encouragement of more expressive writing across the age range and across the whole curriculum. This parallels the position taken by Barnes (1975) who refers to classroom interaction studies which show that talk by the teacher usually makes up the major part of all classroom speech. Classroom interaction most commonly takes the pattern of the teacher asking a question which is answered by the recall of a fact. Barnes therefore recommends that there should be more exploratory talk and writing in classrooms.

However the scope of the WATC approach is much wider than a language acquisition theory, than learning to write. It is concerned with aspects of learning in all parts of the curriculum. Writing is a means of thinking. Writing (or talking) is considered to have a most important role in learning when language is used to represent experience to the self in order to make sense of new information. Hence the importance of the expressive function for trying out ideas and hypotheses tentatively. This language use may be the primary means of learning. From this aspect the WATC approach is a policy for the general educational development of the learner, a policy about writing to learn.

Martin et al. are well aware of the narrower and wider scope of their approach:

> When we began in 1971, we saw the problem as the altering of peoples' view of language. In general people either think of language as something to be corrected and improved, or they take it for granted and just use it . . . . We gradually shifted our attention from how people view language to how they view learning . . . . Changes in the way people see knowledge affects how they see learning and teaching and the learner (ibid., p. 123).

One critic has said that the WATC approach is no more than "the growth and personal development model of English teaching in the 1960s, promoted to a popular interdisciplinary movement" (Williams, 1977:11). The danger is that a view of teaching favored by some English teachers is being imposed on the content teacher. Unless one distinguishes between different strands of WATC, this is quite likely to happen. One end of WATC is a theory about language development. This is about learning to write. Content teaching can be seen from this standpoint as an environment for learning to write and more generally for learning to communicate. Obviously this meets the language teacher's goals and is a field for the language teacher's expertise. The expert on learning to write should be the English teacher. The other end of WATC is a curriculum policy for all subject areas. This is about writing to learn. Content teaching can be seen as an environment where writing and communicating play a role in learning—communicating to learn. Obviously this meets the content teacher's goals and is a field for the content teacher's expertise. The expert on writing to learn chemistry should be the chemistry teacher.

To summarize, content classrooms present a high proportion of teacher talk, and opportunities for student response are limited and tightly controlled. If teachers can provide more opportunities for exploratory student talk and writing, students would have the chance to think through material and make it their own. Student communication about subject matter is an important way of learning because it allows for a process of reflective thinking.

The same policy can benefit second language learners. Their knowledge of English is limited so they are less capable of dealing with large amounts of teacher talk. For the same reason they are less able to express and explore their thinking in English. Their exploratory communication has to be less language laden, but it must still convey their thinking.

READING IN THE CONTENT AREAS

Implications for second language learning in the content classroom can also be drawn from work done in the area of reading across the curriculum (RICA). RICA investigates difficulties students have with reading their content textbooks.

High schools have long been providing instruction in the first phase of reading development: learning how to read . . . . But high schools have not been systematically teaching students to improve in the second phase of reading development: reading and learning from texts or textbooks in content areas. Learning how to read is mastered by most students prior to the eighth grade, but reading to learn from text or any printed material of any length is an ability that continues to develop throughout a person's lifetime . . . . Teachers in such content areas as English, social studies, science and math contribute to both phases of reading development, but mostly to the second. They teach technical vocabulary and concepts, background information, patterns of writing, unique symbols, particular literary devices . . . and specialised modes of inquiry characteristic of their content areas (Singer and Donlan, 1980:3).

'Reading in the content areas' or 'functional reading' is an approach developed for mother tongue speakers. It is particularly prominent in North American work by specialists in reading, and their main recommendation is that some reading instruction should be given by the content teacher in the content class. (This can be done cooperatively, as in one college physics course where a reading professor and the physics professor worked together to pinpoint the difficulties students were having with the textbook.) The approach can be broadly conceived as a variety of techniques of working with a reading passage.

One well-known technique is to make a reading guide to steer the student through the reading of the content. Taking the case of word problems in mathematics, a typical word problem might be:

In a tank there are 100 pounds of a solution of acid and water which is 20% acid. How much water must be evaporated to produce a solution which is 50% acid?

A reading guide would ask a series of questions aimed at taking the reader through at least the following general steps and thus *simulating* the recommended process of reading word problems:

1. Grasping the problem as a whole.
2. Answering the question, What are you to find?
3. Determining what facts you are given to work with.
4. Analyzing the relationship of information given to what you are asked to find, noting both missing and surplus information.
5. Translating the relationships to mathematical terms.

In this way students are guided through the appropriate process in a variety of problem situations.

Earle (1976), from whom this example is taken, gives a forthright statement of the thinking behind the approach:

> Mathematics cannot be studied without reading behaviour as one essential means of subject mastery. Therefore the teacher who expects his students to grow in mathematics must perforce teach the reading of mathematics as it relates to his course of study. The reading teacher cannot possibly select essential vocabulary and understandings, choose mathematical material, set purposes for reading and provide the other necessary guidance to ensure student growth in mathematical reading. By the same token, no mathematics teachers should be expected to teach general reading skills, assign practice reading exercises, or take any classroom time whatever for guidance in reading that is not an integral part of his mathematics instruction . . . . The teaching of reading skills or levels for their own sake results in a subjugation of mathematics content, a condition that mathematics teachers cannot (and should not) tolerate (Earle, 1976:69).

Thus, the reading teacher teaches developmental reading (learning to read) and the mathematics teacher teaches functional reading (reading to learn). In *developmental reading*, the reading materials (e.g., basal readers) are selected to teach basic reading skills, and the language and information is limited because the text is important only as a means to this end. Follow-up activities are aimed at providing development and practice of these skills, e.g., phonics instruction, word recognition, or comprehension work. *Functional reading* materials are essentially the content textbooks themselves, and the aim is to help the student understand the concepts in them. Follow-up activities are aimed at supporting the reading and thinking techniques required to understand a specific aspect of content, such as mathematical word problems. Several useful functional reading techniques can be found in teacher reference books such as Herber (1978) and Singer and Donlan (1980).

Herber (1970, 1978) and a number of reading specialists believe that there are reading and thinking skills which apply across the whole curriculum. These cross-content reading skills are important to the learner because they can be transferred so widely. Herber (1970:122) provides a long list of such non-unique skills, some of which appear in Figure 1.1 on page 17.

Reading skills can therefore be grouped into three sets: developmental reading skills, which are part of a basic ability to read; functional reading skills, which are part of an ability to manage the reading tasks of a particular content area; and cross-content reading skills, which relate to the cognitive processes required by all content areas.

To assist the development of language across the curriculum, these cross-content reading skills must relate to the cognitive processes required by all content areas. However, a crucial problem with cross-content reading skills is that they may not in fact be related to cognitive processes required by all content areas. They may simply be guesses based on the opinions of reading specialists. A way out of this difficulty is to check lists of cross-content reading skills against lists of thinking processes produced by specialists in content areas. (See the lists of thinking processes in content courses in Figure 1.1.)

Content teachers of second language students will find the reading techniques in RICA to be helpful. (But there is no reason why the language teacher should not make use of them too.) RICA was developed in response to the problem that many first language students cannot fully understand their content textbooks. They have learned to read, but find difficulty in reading to learn. RICA's techniques are particularly relevant to second language concerns since the second language student is likely to find content reading tasks even more difficult than the native speaker.

Language and learning in the language class

Teachers in the language classroom can also help the second language learner with the language demands of content learning. Earlier we argued for language teaching which interacts with the communicative environment of the learner, and for many students the most crucial communicative environment is the content classroom. Therefore, we must also look to ESL research and practice for its contribution to cross-curriculum interactive teaching.

Two main ESL teaching approaches have been developed to help second language learners with the language demands of their content classes: English for Specific Purposes and ESL Study Skills. Both of these approaches ultimately aim to help students manage content learning tasks independently. Both have as their goal the teaching of transferable language and thinking skills which apply across the whole curriculum.

English for Specific Purposes selects and teaches language material for chosen communicative environments: the field of medicine, the field of engineering, the field of commerce, and so on. Since many of the teaching materials focus on techniques for working with reading passages from content textbooks, ESP has similarities in approach to 'reading in the content areas' (RICA), and a teacher can combine techniques from both approaches. Further, the historical development of ESP has gone through stages approximately parallel to developmental, functional and cross-content reading skills.

Chronologically we have:

1. *Basic language development.* In *Medicine* (English Language Services, 1966) medical dialogues are chosen and the vocabulary items are used for pronunciation practice and the sentences for pattern drills. Clearly this does not go much beyond the practices of the regular language course. It merely develops a basic ability in the language.

2. *Content comprehension development.* *The Department Store* (Margolis, 1971) offers a reading passage about how a department store operates, followed by comprehension questions. This helps a student through a particular piece of content material, but it is not clear what transferable skills are being developed (aside from technical vocabulary). The material could be improved by drawing on ideas from functional reading techniques.

3. *Cross-content cognitive development.* *English in Mechanical Engineering* (Glendinning, 1974) provides a passage which presents classification of engineering materials. The student is asked to extract the classification from the passage, noting the way classification is expressed, so that he develops the ability to recognize classification in later independent reading. The cross-content reading skill is then transferable to other content areas. This is different from content teaching, for the Glendinning book is not intended to teach engineering. The content material is not information to be learned; its role is to illustrate the content learning task. Many more recent ESP courses are organized around cross-content skills, or cross-content language functions. Lists from Widdowson (1979) and Bates and Dudley-Evans (1976) are given in Figure 1.1. For Bates and Dudley-Evans, description includes properties, shapes, location and structure; measurement covers quantity, proportion, frequency, tendency and probability; and process consists of actions in sequence, method, function/ ability, and cause/effect.

The study skills approach analyzes the learning or study tasks that students face in the content areas, works out what general techniques are required and teaches them. Thus Catterson (1965) offers a study skills list that includes using graphic materials, using book parts (tables of contents, indexes), using sources (card catalogues, encyclopedias), organization perceived (e.g. reorganizing paragraph patterns), organization produced (e.g. making outlines, taking notes). The list is also given in Figure 1.1. Many ESL teachers take students through a study task as a method by which to teach study skills for content learning. A study task, such as writing a term paper or an answer to a question, is then used to teach students how to gather and select information (critical reading); how to organize the material (reflective thinking); and how to express it (thoughtful writing).

While study skills are taught in combination with ESP and with RICA, unfortunately there is no unifying framework linking all three.

Part A of Figure 1.1 gives a list of general skills and language functions for content areas gathered from ESP, study skills and RICA. The skills and functions are based on

Figure 1.1

	A. Language Academic Communication And Thinking				B. Content Thinking Processes in Content Courses	
	RICA	ESP	ESP	Study Skills	Science	Social Studies
	Herber (1978)	Widdowson (ed) (1979)	Bates and Dudley-Evans (1976)	Catterson (1965)	A.A.A.S. (1970)	Durkin (1969)
	Cause/effect	Generalization	Description	Using graphic materials	Observing	Listing
	Comparison/ contrast	Description	Measurement	Using book parts	Using space/time relationships	Grouping and labelling
	Time order	Definition	Process	Using sources	Classifying	Inferring and generalizing
	Simple listing	Classification		Organization perceived	Using numbers	
		Hypotheses		Organization produced	Measuring	
					Communicating, predicting, inferring, controlling variables, interpreting data, formulating hypotheses, defining operationally, experimenting	

the language teacher's knowledge of language and discourse, and reflect the language teacher's interests. The lists are designed to serve the learner's language needs. However, while they reflect our aim of obtaining cross-content thinking skills and language, we cannot be sure that the language lists are, in Herber's words, "cognitive skills appropriate to all disciplines."

Part B of Figure 1.1 contains lists of thinking processes derived from inquiry courses in two content areas, social studies and science. The lists are based upon the content teacher's knowledge of the content disciplines, and reflect the content teacher's interests. These lists are designed to serve the learner's content needs.

Commonalities between the two parts of Figure 1.1 clearly exist. However, if we are to have an integrated approach to language and learning across the curriculum, a common organizing framework is needed. Although this is a difficult task, it is a necessary one. Lacking an organizing framework, students are forced to integrate the work in their language classes and content classes on their own, without any guidance. What for teachers is simply difficult, may prove impossible for students.

1.4 SUMMARY AND CONCLUSION

To pull together the strands of this review of language teaching and content teaching, let us return to the traditional view where language teaching and content teaching were considered as two distinctly different activities.

When we move beyond this view, and language is regarded as a medium of learning, we can see that language learning takes place both in the content classroom and the language classroom. Language learning in the communicative environment of the *content* classroom furthers the goals of language teaching by offering a context for language. It provides language use in a context of communication about important subject matter. Language ceases to be taught in isolation. At the same time, language learning in the *language* classroom can further the goals of content teaching by offering learners help with the language of the thinking processes and the structure or shape of content.

Regarding language as a medium of learning naturally leads to a cross-curriculum perspective. We have seen that reading specialists contrast learning to read with reading to learn. Writing specialists contrast learning to write with writing to learn. Similarly, language education specialists should distinguish between language learning and using language to learn. Helping students use language to learn requires us to look beyond the language domain to all subject areas and to look beyond language learning to education in general. Outside the isolated language classroom students learn language and content at the same time. Therefore we need a broad perspective which integrates language and content learning.

It is clear that an organizing framework for teaching language across the curriculum is needed. Moreover, the characteristics of a framework can be identified. We need to:

1. *Develop an organizing framework of language and thinking skills which apply*

across the curriculum. We need to go beyond techniques which help a student understand a particular lesson; we need to help the student to acquire the ability to develop this understanding independently. This calls for general language and thinking skills which can be transferred. The organizing framework must help the student to connect work in the language class and the content class.

2. *Improve communication of subject matter*. This is not only a concern of second language students, but also for first language students. It is a concern at all levels of education, from elementary to university, wherever subject matter is communicated. Communication of subject matter is fundamental to education, and the framework should assist it.

3. *Find strategies for developing the language skills in this general framework*. This, of course, is of special importance to the language teacher.

4. *Find strategies for developing the thinking skills in this general framework*. This is of special interest to the content teacher who is not only interested in conveying information but also in ways of thinking about information.

In the next chapter we will introduce a framework which responds to these needs.

EXERCISES FOR
CHAPTER ONE*

Awareness and attitudes

1. Survey the languages that students know. Students and teachers list the languages spoken, written and understood by the whole school population. This can be shown in a chart indicating the range of multilingualism within a school. Any institution or workplace can surveyed in this way.

2. Survey the problems of ESL teachers. In a national survey, Ashworth (1975) asked the question: "What do you consider to be the major problem facing you as a teacher of ESL students?" Responses included the following topics: lack of time, class make-up, curriculum and materials, administrators and classroom teachers, teaching difficulties (e.g., the slow learner) and the social adjustment of the learner. Try the same question on a group of ESL teachers, noting the details of the answers.

3. Survey problems of ESL learners. Ashworth (1975) asked teachers: "What do you consider to be the major problem facing your ESL students?" Responses were classified into education, language, and culture. Ask the question of some ESL teachers. In addition, or alternatively, ask the question of a group of ESL students.

4. Profile a typical ESL learner. A representative student is identified and described. Age, life history, schooling, family background and home situation, interests, attitudes to education, aspirations may all be relevant. Of particular interest are ways in which the student differs from the typical English-speaking student. Several different profiles can show contrasts between different groups of ESL learners. An important question is:

* The stimulus for a number of these exercises was Whitney (1982).

what social roles does the ESL learner have to perform in English, in addition to the role of language learner?

5. Take the role of the second language learner. Teachers become the students in a lesson which is taught in a language unfamiliar to them. This may be a beginning lesson in Swahili, for instance, taught by the direct method, where no English is used. Participants usually find that this is a very rewarding experience. It is often helpful for the learners to note down their feelings during the lesson for discussion and analysis later. Sometimes feelings of fear and frustration are prominent. Another aspect of the experience is to describe how communication is managed between teacher and students: what did the teacher want to convey, how did the teacher try to convey it, and what did the students understand. This experience can be given a new twist by making it more than a language lesson and attempting to teach content in the unfamiliar language. Here the participant has to play the role of the language learner and the role of the student of content. Examples have included teaching mathematics in Cantonese and computer flowcharting in Swiss German. This can be correspondingly more difficult for all concerned. Particularly in this case, it is good to tape or video the lesson for later replay and analysis in order to capture all the details of the process.

6. Review the role of the ESL teacher. Aside from the role of classroom teacher, what is the role of the ESL teacher as a "good colleague" (Whitney 1982), communicating with other teachers in the interests of the ESL student? What is the role of the ESL teacher as a general advocate for the ESL student? Pick an ESL teacher (perhaps yourself) and list some of the things done in these roles. How important were they? How much time did they take?

7. Survey teacher attitudes. How do non-ESL teachers feel about ESL students? How do they feel about ESL teachers (and vice-versa)? How do they see the role of the ESL teacher? What kind of cooperation is desirable between the ESL teacher and the non-ESL teacher? What are some of the pitfalls? These can be delicate issues. Ashworth (1975) approached these problems by asking ESL teachers: "How well do the other teachers in your school accept ESL students?" Answers mentioned factors such as class size and workload, lack of experience with ESL students, and cultural differences and prejudice.

8. Survey student attitudes. How do ESL learners feel about language classes? How do they feel about content classes? What do they see to be the most helpful aspects of their language classes? What is the least helpful? What language needs do they have that are not being met? What communication problems do they have in content classes? How do they handle the problems? What content classes are easy to deal with? What content classes are difficult to deal with? Do they mix with non-ESL students? How well do the other students in the school accept the ESL students? These questions can be asked of ESL teachers or of ESL students.

Analyzing the content learning environment

9. Observe a content lesson. Observe a content lesson presented to a class containing ESL learners. Describe the language demands on the ESL student. Look for the various language skills required of the learner: speaking, listening, reading and writing. How is the

lesson organized? Is there group work? How much student talk occurs? What are the students required to do? How are they evaluated?

10. Analyze a typical student task. Analyze the language demands of a typical student task or assignment in a content area. Students often bring problems of this kind to a language, reading, or study skills center if they have access to one. What reading, writing, or study skills are required? What difficulties does the student have?

11. Evaluate textbooks and materials. What do ESL students like and dislike about a content book they use? What does the content teacher like or dislike about it? What use do the students make of the book? What kind of materials do they prefer? Why?

12. Interview a content teacher. Interview a content teacher about a content course. What style of teaching does the teacher prefer (lecture, group discussion, student activities..)? What are the special requirements of the course? Ask about curriculum guides, textbooks, worksheets, assignments, examinations. Where does the course make its heaviest language demands on ESL students? Where would help by the ESL teacher be most valuable?

Analyzing and adapting materials and situations

13. Analyze content materials, I. Pick a content lesson (e.g., from a textbook) or any content material or activity that is difficult for the ESL learners you are interested in. Discuss the language aspect of the material. Is it understandable to ESL learners? How could you help ESL students grasp the teaching point? What kinds of difficulties does it present? What student aids and student activities would be helpful? (Pictures, diagrams, hands-on experience, role playing and other student activities, study guides . . .). Do the central points have to be highlighted more carefully? Would opportunities for preview or review help?

14. Analyze content materials, II. Pick content material or a content activity that is likely to be manageable for your ESL learners. What makes it understandable, manageable, or motivating? (For example is the material practical or familiar?) What student activities are involved? How can ESL learners communicate their understanding to the teacher? What would make the activity progressively more challenging? If you were to use this material as the basis of a language lesson, how would you develop it?

15. Analyze language materials, I. Language teaching materials almost always deal with some topic, or at least talk about something. In other words, they relate language learning and topic information in some way: for example, adjectives may be taught by describing physical objects in the classroom. Looking at this more carefully can be a helpful source of strategies for making systematic connections between content learning and language learning. Pick a language lesson which is not specially designed to present content. Discuss the content aspect of the lesson. What information or activity is presented? What do the students have to do with this? Is the content trivial, useful, interesting, familiar? Why was it chosen? Suggest ways of improving or expanding the content aspect so that it is more useful to the student. Could you substitute "real" content, like describing a map or describing equipment, without changing the language aspect too much? Finnochiaro and Bonomo (1973, pp. 261–266) give a handy list, matching language structures with classroom "situations," such as clocks, calendars, and maps, and they

suggest that it is desirable to present an item initially in the classroom situation and then fan out into the wider community.

16. Analyze language materials, II. Pick a language lesson which has been designed to contain the type of content that could appear in a content lesson (e.g., English for specific purposes material, reading in the content areas material, or material for secondary schools like "Scope Stage II.") Give details of the content information and activities and of the language points and activities. What was the plan for combining the two? Do you think the authors chose the content first and made the language fit in or was it the other way around? Or does the combination seem to work naturally? The aim of the exercise is to find some strategies helpful in planning language teaching for the ESL content learner.

CHAPTER ONE
SUGGESTED READINGS

Ashworth, N. 1975. *Immigrant Children and Canadian Schools.* Toronto: McLelland and Stewart. A national survey of immigrant ESL students in Canada. Chapter 8 discusses problems facing ESL students, including achievement in subject areas.

Brown, D. 1979. *Mother Tongue to English: The Young Child in the Multicultural School.* Cambridge: Cambridge U.P. Aims to make teachers and all involved in the education of young children aware of the special needs of those who come from ethnic minority groups, and to give positive and practical help in meeting those needs. Particular attention is paid to the needs of children whose mother tongue is not English. Presents a detailed case study of two Bengali-speaking children in normal classes in an infant school.

Chamot, A. 1983. "Toward a Functional ESL Curriculum in the Elementary School." *TESOL Quarterly* 17, 3:459–471. A proposal for an ESL curriculum in the elementary school for language minority children which emphasizes the cognitive and academic skills needed to study school subjects in English.

Cohen, A. and M. Swain. 1976. "Bilingual education: The "Immersion Model." *TESOL Quarterly* 10, 1:45–54. Compares and contrasts the immersion situation of students studying French in Canada and English in the U.S.A.

Cummins, J. 1981. *Bilingualism and Minority-Language Children.* Toronto: Ontario Institute for Studies in Education. A short, readable account of issues, research findings, theory, and practice.

Early, M., C. Thew, and P. Wakefield. Forthcoming, 1985. *ESL Instruction via the Regular Curriculum: A Framework and Resource Book.* Victoria, B.C., Canada. Ministry of Education. A resource guide for ESL and content area teachers based on the approach described in this book. Presents a clear overview, provides many model lessons, and illustrates the connection between language curricula and subject area curricula.

Herber, H. (ed.). 1965. *Developing Study Skills in Secondary Schools.* Newark, Delaware: International Reading Association. A series of essays on study skills in secondary schools for first language students, with an introductory overview.

Herber, H. 1978. *Teaching Reading in the Content Areas.* (2nd ed.). New Jersey: Prentice-Hall. A systematic account of reading in the content areas for both the elementary school and the secondary school. Gives a broad picture of the ideas behind the approach recommended and applies these ideas to the structure of the chapters of the book itself.

Jupp, T. and S. Hodlin. 1975. *Industrial English*. London: Heinemann. Provides a systematic and fully documented approach to functional teaching for special purposes, particularly in work situations. Based on a large amount of experience in industrial language teaching. Shows the importance of cultural factors and the damaging effects of communication failures in work situations. Describes an elementary English course easily open to adaptation and variation.

Krashen, S. 1982. *Principles and Practice in Second Language Acquisition*. Oxford: Pergamon. Examines the relationship between practices in second language teaching and what is known about the process of second language acquisition and presents Krashen's 'Monitor Theory' based on the distinction he draws between acquisition and learning. Concludes that a solution to language teaching lies not so much in exotic new methods but rather in the full utilization of the most important resources—native speakers of the language—in real communication.

Mackay, R. and A. Mountford (eds.). 1978. *English for Specific Purposes*. London: Longman. A series of essays which survey the problem, outline various approaches to ESP textbook design, and present case studies of syllabi and materials. Underlying theoretical and descriptive principles governing functionally-oriented syllabi are related to the practical questions of design and materials production.

Marland, M. 1977. *Language Across the Curriculum*. London: Heinemann. A series of essays discussing a whole-school language policy, the components of a policy, and how it might be implemented.

Martin, N. et al. 1976. *Writing and Learning Across the Curriculum 11–16*. London: Ward Lock. This book arose from the work of the British Schools Council Writing across the Curriculum Project. Initially seen as a book about writing across the curriculum by first language learners 11–16 years old, it also says a great deal about talking and reading and thinking and learning as these processes take place in secondary schools. The authors suggest that too much of writing and talking in school is used to test what children know and too little is concerned with enabling them to learn and make sense of things for themselves.

Paulston, C. 1980. *Bilingual Education: Theories and Issues*. Rowley, Mass: Newbury House. Discusses social issues in bilingual education and conflicting findings in research.

Robinson, P. 1980. *ESP: English for Specific Purposes*. Oxford: Pergamon Press. A monograph which reviews the field of English for specific purposes.

Singer, H. and D. Donlan. 1980. *Reading and Learning from Text*. Boston: Little, Brown. Presents a school-wide program for reading in the secondary school. Deals with reading in English, Social Studies, Science, and Mathematics and includes sections on talking and writing. Contains a large number of practical techniques explained in detail.

Swain, M. and S. Lapkin. 1982. *Evaluating Bilingual Education: A Canadian Case Study*. Clevedon, Avon: Multilingual Matters. A review of a decade of research in Canada on bilingual education.

Wakefield, P. et al. 1981. *English as a Second Language/Dialect Resources Book for K-12*. Victoria, B.C.: Ministry of Education. A general resource book containing a section on language across the curriculum with model lessons.

Whitney, N. et al. 1980. *Language Across the Curriculum: Progress Report*. London: Ealing College of Higher Education. A report of a cooperative project in language across the curriculum by a team of language specialists and teachers from a multicultural high school. Contains details of practical problems and approaches.

Widdowson, H. 1978. *Teaching Language as Communication*. Oxford: Oxford University Press. An account of the communicative approach to language teaching with particular emphasis on language as discourse.

Williams, J. 1977. *Learning to Write, or Writing to Learn?* Slough: National Foundation for Educational Research. A criticism of the work of the writing across the curriculum movement.

Yorkey, R. 1970. *Study Skills for Studies of English as a Second Language*. New York: McGraw-Hill. A study skills textbook for ESL students.

Chapter 2

A Knowledge Framework for Activities

2.1 INTRODUCTION

Our review of language and content teaching in Chapter 1 pointed to the need to develop an organizing framework for language and thinking skills across the curriculum. In this chapter we will develop an organizing framework and show how teachers can use it to improve communication, thinking, and language across the curriculum.

This organizing framework will be based on the concept of an activity, which is central to education, since education initiates the learner into the public activities of his or her society. The organizing framework to be developed here is not only based on the idea of an activity, it is also intended to be a guide to the structure of knowledge across the curriculum. But because the structure of knowledge is abstract, we use graphics to represent it and communicate about it. We can begin by showing how the framework applies to the teaching of topics or themes.

Teaching topics or themes

How would you teach a topic of worthwhile or interesting information to a class of ESL students using English as the medium of instruction? What would be a broad, general plan for doing this which could cover both the more practical and the more theoretical aspects of topics, and at the same time be easily adapted to various needs?

If you are a content teacher, this is the problem of teaching your subject area to an ESL class. It is the problem of how to adapt a lesson which had been successful with a class of English-speaking students. Martinez (1984) suggests three points:

1. Cut down your teaching objectives by half, concentrating on the most important ones.

2. Provide for preview and review.

3. Use visuals and graphics.

As a subject specialist you want to convey essential subject information to your students, but in addition you want to develop their thinking skills.

If you are a language teacher, this is the problem of organizing a lesson around a theme or topic rather than around a grammar point. As a language teacher you are skilled at communicating with ESL students, but your special concern is to do more than teach information. You want to find ways to help the students' language development.

There are therefore three general aims:

1. To make classroom communication simpler and clearer; to lower the language barrier.

2. To highlight opportunities for language development.

3. To highlight opportunities for developing general thinking skills.

The approach used here supports these aims by making the structure of the topic information as clear as possible.

A simple example:
a museum tour

Museums and other public exhibits are fine resources for learning through field trips. But for ESL learners they present all the problems of teaching a topic. For instance, how can the language barrier be overcome?

One group of teachers tackled this problem by writing a teacher's resource book for field trips by ESL students to a local museum (Chappell et al., 1981). The book gives a description for the teacher of the museum's exhibits and information, shows ways to improve the ESL students's access to this information, and outlines a number of language development activities.

One part of the resource book deals with the museum exhibit which presents the sequence of early sea exploration of the Pacific northwest coast from 1741. The museum displays show a rich variety of objects: sea-otter pelts, Russian coins, Spanish armor, a model of a British sailing ship. An important goal is for the students to grasp the general sequence of historical events which organizes these details into a coherent whole.

For this purpose the resource book contains a simple chart which outlines the main events in table form. (See Figure 2.1) Some parts of the chart are deliberately left blank. The student views the exhibit with a copy of the chart and fills in the missing information in the chart as an information gathering activity. Back in the classroom the student produces an oral or written report using the chart as a basis.

The chart can be used flexibly in a variety of ways. For example, leaving more parts of the chart blank makes it more challenging to fill in; the students can be asked

Figure 2.1
Early Explorers

Who?	When?	How?	Where?
Russian-Bering		by sea	to Alaska and Aleutians
Spanish-San Joset	1774		from Mexico to 55° N.
English—?	1776	by sea	to Nootka Sound

to locate the sources of their information in the exhibit; they can gather their own information from the exhibit and develop their own information charts.

The chart technique can be used for a large variety of topics. A chart can be developed for very many kinds of information gathering activities by a wide range of ESL students, both in the classroom and outside of the classroom. It is not only a simple type of worksheet; it is also an easy way to present the information that the student has gathered. It can also be used as a step in developing oral or written work.

Every teacher is familiar with the use of charts. The key difference in the approach here is that the teachers first decided on the central issue, the sequence of events, and then designed the chart. They analyzed the museum material, chose the most important structure in the material, and designed a graphic to convey it.

The information chart therefore meets the three aims of the general plan for working with a topic:

1. It makes communication clearer and lowers the language barrier. For the information gathering task it is easier for a student to work with a chart than to answer a list of written questions. When the student has to give a report, the completed chart is a better support than student notes.

2. It is an opportunity for the development of the language of sequence. The chart can be developed into a paragraph of sequence.

3. It develops general thinking or process skills, as students are encouraged to look for the sequence of historical events. The students are guided to sequence their information into the main historical events in early exploration. They can then discuss their interpretation of these events. In addition, they are alerted to looking for the time order of historical information in general.

To sum up, the museum information chart shows the idea behind the approach. The authors decided on the main knowledge structure of the museum information—sequence in time—and designed a graphic which showed this simply and clearly.

2.2 ORGANIZING INFORMATION

An example from automobile insurance

Finding the main structures of knowledge in a topic is an important task in planning to teach the topic. The approach used in the simple case of the museum tour can be applied and extended to more complex examples. The next example contains a number of different structures of knowledge that fit together into a pattern. It illustrates a framework for organizing topic information that applies to language and thinking across the curriculum.

The Westcoast Reader is a graded newspaper for adults who are learning to read English. Its readership includes English speakers who are in Adult Basic Education classes and also school-age learners as early as grade four. It was designed to provide interesting, relevant information about local and national issues and to assist in the development of reading skills and of language learning generally. Most of the material is adapted from articles in newspapers, and it often devotes part of an issue to a single topic.

In one issue the topic was auto insurance and crashes. A government agency that dealt in automobile insurance agreed to provide financial support and to make its public education material freely available. The task of the editorial team was to select, organize, and adapt this material and to design follow-up language activities for the classroom. The team used a general framework that could be applied to many topics.

The first job was to organize the mass of material and information on the topic, such as studies of the causes of automobile crashes and procedures for making insurance claims. We reviewed the material and made a list of the main subtopics, such as types of insurance and claims procedures. We looked for an action situation which was central to the topic and chose the crash situation. This was expanded into a story of a typical case designed to illustrate the main subtopics. It became a photostory of a person insuring a car, having a crash, and reporting the incident. (See Figure 2.2.) Then we took the information on the various subtopics and produced short, simple written articles on each. Where appropriate, the agency's charts and diagrams illustrated the articles. (See Figure 2.3 for a facsimile.)

The teachers' notes for the reading and language development activities pointed out that the photostory had been designed to serve as the core of the topic, with all the articles relating to it. The photostory supplied a specific example while the background articles gave general information and covered other possibilities than the ones that were shown in the story. It was suggested that the students first discuss the story and then read the articles. As a final evaluation they could be asked to rewrite part of the photostory.

From Figures 2.2 and 2.3 we can extract the main structures of knowledge in the insurance topic. From the photostory (Figure 2.2) we can see that the information about the typical case can be divided into description, sequence, and choice.

1. *Description.* Each picture presents a relevant scene like buying insurance or having a crash. The flow of events has been divided into separate scenes or descriptions.

2. *Sequence.* The story shows a natural sequence of development. The characters have a crash, report the accident, make an insurance claim. The pictures show a time sequence.

3. *Choice.* People involved in crashes have to make certain choices or decisions. For example, after a crash it is necessary to decide about reporting the accident to the police. This is shown in photo #5. Choices are points where a story could develop in different directions.

Description, sequence, and choice can be found in any story, process, or procedure which illustrates a particular case. A particular case presents specific, practical knowledge.

Now consider the newspaper articles in Figure 2.3. The information in the background articles reveals three structures: classification, principles, and evaluation.

1. *Classification.* The "Autoplan" article presents a classification of the different types of insurance available.

2. *Principles.* The "Causes of Accidents" article discusses causes of car crashes such as road conditions. A cause-effect relation is one kind of principle. Other kinds would include means-end relations (ways to drive safely), and rules (rules of the road).

3. *Evaluation.* "Bad News for Bad Drivers" shows how driving is evaluated. Drivers who cause accidents (bad drivers) are penalized. Safe drivers (good drivers) receive an insurance discount.

Background information on any topic will usually include classification, principles, and evaluation. Background knowledge is general, theoretical knowledge. It applies to many particular examples.

The photostory can be used to develop the language of description, sequence, and choice. Each photo can be described individually; the sequence of two or more photos can be narrated; and with certain photos, the students can discuss choices.

The background articles can be used to develop the language of classification, principles, and evaluation: for example, types of insurance are classified; causes of accidents are indicated; and bad drivers are evaluated. To take the article on car insurance as one instance, the types of insurance mentioned can be shown in the classification tree given in Figure 2.4 on page 34.

This classification tree can be given to students with some of the information left out. After reading the article, they could fill in the blanks. More advanced students might draw the tree after having read the article, or conversely, given the tree, turn it back into written discourse.

Figure 2.2

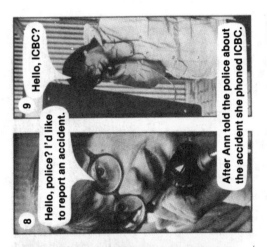

After Ann told the police about the accident she phoned ICBC.

Let's park our cars in a safe place first.

At the claim centre an estimator will estimate the damage. Ann can then get her car repaired.

The drivers must call the police because the damage is over $400. Each person must also report to ICBC. ICBC and the police decided that Gino caused the crash. Gino's insurance will go up. The police may charge him. Sometimes a driver who caused a crash has to go to court and sometimes even to jail. For example, a drunk driver may have to go to jail.

Photography by Joshua Berson

Photo courtesy ICBC

Figure 2.3

the westcoast reader extra

SPECIAL ISSUE ON CAR INSURANCE   JANUARY 1983

Bad news for bad drivers

✔✔In 1983 bad drivers in B.C. have to pay a lot more for their insurance than in 1982.

The steps on the right explain the new cost of Autoplan insurance for B.C. drivers. The cost of your insurance starts with a base rate. The average base rate in B.C. is $500. This cost can go up or down depending on how safely you drive.

For each accident you cause your insurance premium will increase by three steps. A driver moves down the scale only one step at a time. Each step down will take one full year of safe driving. To encourage people high on the scale to improve their driving, their premium will go back to the base rate after three years without accidents.

Example: Mr. X is paying the base rate ($500) for his insurance. He causes an accident and moves three steps up the scale. His insurance will be about $650. If he has another accident his insurance will be about $875. After three years without accidents, Mr. X will be back at the base rate.

There is also a discount for safe drivers. In 1983 a driver with a base rate of $500 who has caused no accidents for a minimum of 4 years, will pay $325 for his or her insurance. If Mr. X, from the example above, continues to drive safely, he can move, one step at a time, down the discount steps. It pays to be a safe driver.

Vancouver Sun

Autoplan's Claim-Rated Scale

425% $2125
400% $2000
350% $1750
325% $1625
300% $1500
250% $1250
225% $1125
200% $1000
175% $875
160% $800
145% $725
130% $650
120% $600
110% $550
100% $500
90% $450
80% $400
70% $350
65% $325

Causes of accidents

✔People cause most car crashes. About 90 per cent of crashes happen because a driver makes an error.

Sometimes the weather or road conditions cause accidents. For example, the roads may be slippery. A few crashes happen because the car isn't working properly. For example, it may have bad brakes or poor tires. You should check and repair your car regularly.

But most accidents happen because people make mistakes. Here are some of the reasons for many car crashes.

• The driver has been drinking alcohol.
• The driver forgets to look at the other cars, or he looks but he doesn't see them.
• The driver goes too fast.
• The driver is thinking about something so he doesn't pay attention.

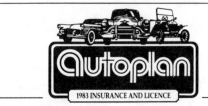

1983 INSURANCE AND LICENCE

✔✔ICBC means Insurance Corporation of British Columbia. It is a Crown Corporation (big, government company).

The main part of ICBC is car insurance. This insurance is called Autoplan. Everyone with a car in B.C. must have Autoplan insurance. This is the law.

All cars must have $100,000 (compulsory) Third Party Liability insurance. That means you are protected if you cause injury or damage to others (third parties). Many people buy extra Third Party Liability insurance. This is a good idea. It doesn't cost much more, and it will provide up to $1,000,000 in case of a very bad crash.

B.C. senior citizens get a discount on their Autoplan insurance. The discount is about 25 per cent of the premium for the compulsory Third Party Liability insurance.

You can also get other (optional) insurance coverage in case you damage your own car. There are four kinds of "own damage" insurance. They are Collision, Comprehensive, Specified Perils, and All Perils. You must decide which is best for you. Ask your nearest Autoplan agent for advice.

How much you pay for your insurance depends on what kind of insurance you want, and whether you are a safe driver. People who have many accidents pay a lot more for their insurance than safe drivers. People who use their cars only for pleasure pay less for insurance than people who use their cars for work. If you buy some "own damage" insurance, the price depends on how much deductible you want, and the kind of car you have. The deductible is the amount of money you pay to the bodyshop if you caused the crash that damaged your car. It is usually $100-$200.

You have to renew your Autoplan insurance on the same date each year. You can do that at a Motor Licence Office or at any Autoplan agent.

Figure 2.4
Classification Tree for Automobile Insurance

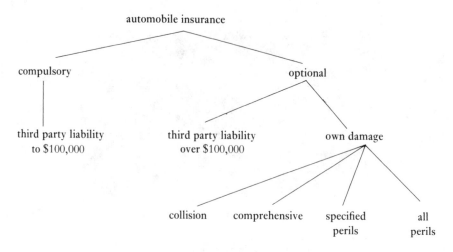

A general procedure for organizing information

The procedure taken with the topic was as follows:

1. Get an overall sense of the topic and then divide it into specific, particular, practical cases and examples, and into general, theoretical background knowledge.
2. Choose a specific example. Present it as a picture story or other suitable form such as a demonstration, a drama, a student experience, a film, a process, or a narrative.
3. Present the background knowledge as charts or tables or other suitable forms such as reading passages or short lectures.
4. Use the particular case to illustrate the general principles and use general principles to help the student interpret the particular case.
5. Use the knowledge structures of the particular case (description, sequence, and choice) to develop corresponding thinking skills and language skills. Do the same for the knowledge structures of the general information (classification, principles, and evaluation). If you use graphics as a center of organization and as a guide to student activities, this will often happen naturally, without a great deal of planning on the teacher's part.

Although in this example the emphasis is on the teacher presenting information rather than on the student gathering and expressing information, either emphasis is possible. A picture story or a classification can be created either by the teacher or by the students. Graphics can be used either way.

2.3 THE KNOWLEDGE FRAMEWORK

The key to this approach to topics is to find the main structures of topic information. This calls for a framework which applies to a wide range of topics. This framework for topic information is shown in Figure 2.5. It is a guide to the structure of knowledge across the curriculum. The framework is of central importance to our discussion throughout this book, and later chapters will develop different aspects of it.

The car insurance example fits into the framework as in Figure 2.6. The photostory goes with the specific, practical side of the framework and the articles and charts go with the general, theoretical side of the framework. (See also section 2.4.)

The specific, practical side of the framework divides into description, sequence, and choice (decision making). Any photostory divides into description (single pictures), sequence (a sequence of pictures), and choice (alternative possible pictures). The same division can be made for any narrative or process.

Figure 2.5
General Framework for Knowledge Structures

ACTIVITY

	Specific, Practical	General, Theoretical	
	(Action situation)	(Background knowledge)	
Description			Concepts and Classification
Sequence			Principles
Choice			Evaluation

Figure 2.6

Car Insurance Example in the General Framework

ACTIVITY: CAR INSURANCE

	Action situation (see Figure 2.2)	Background knowledge (see Figure 2.3)	
Description	any story picture e.g., picture 3, 'the crash'	article: "Autoplan"	Concepts and Classification
Sequence	any sequence of pictures e.g., pictures 2,3,4	article: "Causes of Accidents"	Principles
Choice	any decision picture e.g., picture 5	article: "Bad News for Bad Drivers"	Evaluation

The general, theoretical side of the framework divides into concepts and classification, principles, and evaluation. The general background information for most topics can be divided in this way. With the car insurance material, it was not so much a matter of finding information to fill these categories; rather, it was a matter of recognizing the categories in existing material and then taking advantage of them. In other words, general information may already be naturally organized into these categories.

We can explore the framework through a set of questions the teacher can ask when analyzing topic material. And these questions can also be adapted as a basis for guiding student questions about a topic. Essentially, the knowledge structure of a topic is reflected in the questions people ask about it.

A. *Specific, practical aspect:* find particular examples, specific cases within the topic. What would a film about the topic show?

1. Description: who, what, where? What persons, materials, equipment, items, settings?

2. Sequence: what happens? What happens next? What is the plot? What are the processes, procedures, or routines?

3. Choice: what are the choices, conflicts, alternatives, dilemmas, decisions?

B. *General, theoretical aspect:* what are the general concepts, principles and values in the topic material?

1. Classification: what concepts apply? How are they related to each other?

2. Principles: what principles are there? (Cause-effect, means-end, methods and techniques, rules, norms, strategies).

3. Evaluation: what values and standards are appropriate? What counts as good or bad? What are typical reasons for choosing one object or course of action over another? What are usual aims and goals?

The next two sections give examples which show how this approach to topics can be used to adapt existing materials. The first section shows adaptation for language teaching purposes; the second section shows adaptation for content teaching purposes. In both cases the strategy is to identify important knowledge structures.

Using the knowledge framework:
the example of nutrition

Sometimes topic material can be found that is ready-made. It can be presented to students with only a little adaptation; it is already organized into a general pattern or structure, and it contains graphics which reflect this structure. For the language teacher the remaining task is to plan language development activities. A convenient strategy is to design these around the graphics provided.

Government and educational agencies are a rich source of such material. Often free and often with highly professional visual aids, this material can be selected and adapted by the teacher. For example, the British Columbia Dairy Foundation provides a set of materials on the topic of nutrition for use in schools. The graphics are excellent, and the overall structure corresponds quite well to the general framework given here. Teachers at Vancouver School Board have assembled material like this into a resource book for ESL teachers: *English Through Nutrition* (Vancouver School Board, 1980). It uses nutrition materials produced by the British Columbia Dairy Foundation and gives accompanying language activities, with the double aim of providing nutrition information to ESL students K-12 and offering systematic language development for all levels of language learners. Some examples of how these teachers use preexisting visuals and graphics are:

- Pictures of individual fruits and vegetables to be used as flash cards (description).

- Pictures of food groups (classification).

- A picture of the digestive process: *How a Hamburger Turns into You* (sequence).

- Instructions for testing for nutrients (e.g., for vitamins), and charts to fill out for the test results (cause-effect).

Related language development activities then include using the food pictures to play board games like 'Snakes and Ladders' (description) or card games like 'Pyramid' (classification); linking the digestive process to its effects on growth by having the students measure themselves earlier and later in the year; and playing 'Yummy Rummy' with food playing cards (the object of the game is to get a 'balanced hand' made up one card from each of the four food groups). An important extra element in the book is cultural exploration; there is a section on understanding Chinese and Indian culture through food.

Another way of making a language and content resource book is shown by *ESL through Food Skills* (Vancouver School Board, 1981). This is a modification of a Vancouver School Board Home Economics Curriculum Resource Book, with language activities added and visuals and graphics included from various commercial sources. Notable is its use of pictures of safety hazards in the kitchen and the home (decision-making), label symbols for dangerous substances—'danger', 'warning', and 'caution'—and charts for standards of good muffins, biscuits, and cakes (evaluation), all with appropriate language development activities.

Using the knowledge framework:
modifying a social studies unit

A content teacher can organize information not only to present material more clearly to ESL students, but particularly to bring out the structure of the topic and aid the development of thinking skills.

A seventh grade social studies unit was modified for ESL students in this way by Meryl Arnott (Arnott, unpublished), who is a teacher of both ESL and social studies. The unit, 'Marooned,' (Canadian Social Services, 1973) develops an understanding of culture. The students imagine themselves to be marooned on an uninhabited desert island with no adults, no articles from their technological world, and no hope of rescue. In order to survive they must create a culture. In working through the exercises and activities that lead to building this culture the students learn about their new environment, discover ways of meeting their physical, mental, and social needs, and make decisions about issues that arise.

The motivational activity for the unit is a series of adventures beginning with a school trip and ending with the students being marooned. This was supported by a picture story presented on an overhead transparency. The students then work through booklets of information about the environment of the island, and they are helped to summarize these details into various kinds of resources. They fill in a classification chart listing the resources under headings like: Resource—coconut, Description—palm tree with nuts, Location—along the beaches, Kind—plant, Use—food. Next they discuss ways of meeting their needs such as physical ones that have to be supported by the resources of the island. Here they fill in means-end charts relating resources to needs like: Material—coconut shell, Tool—water container, Use—holds water, Need—food and water. Finally the students are presented with various issues that arise on the island. In order to decide on a solution the students have to clarify their own values in relation to each issue. One issue is the kind of government the castaways should set up: political equality, political inequality, or no government at all. The students need to be clear about the alternatives, express their evaluation of each, and arrive at a group decision. An evaluation chart presents the alternatives clearly and leaves room for the students' evaluation of each one.

To reach the inquiry and thinking goals of this unit, the students must do more than create an imaginary culture. They must develop an understanding of culture in general. This means that they must see the general pattern of what they are doing; they must see the links between environment and resources, resources and need, social issues and social organization as matters which apply to any culture. The charts were designed to help these goals by bringing out this pattern clearly and simply. Most students, English speakers as well as ESL, could benefit from this technique.

Review

Using graphics, thematic units can be developed to present information on a topic and also offer opportunities for systematic work with language. The same is true for teacher resource books and for modifications of standard curriculum materials for second language learners. An advantage of using graphics as an organizing center is that it helps teachers use already existing materials. However, it is not enough merely to gather graphics on a topic. The graphics should be selected to reflect important aspects of the topic's structure. In other words, decide on the structure of the topic, and use graphics to show this structure clearly.

This is a very important point which is extremely easy to overlook. It is different from the simple use of graphics as an aid to communication. The simple use of graphics is almost universal in teaching. Presenting the structure of knowledge is more difficult, but much more rewarding, both for the content teacher and for the language teacher.

Every teacher is interested in communicating the structure of knowledge because every teacher wants students to be able to transfer their learning beyond the immediate lesson. The content teacher wants students to learn detailed information in a particular lesson, but beyond that, the teacher wants to convey the 'shape' of subject matter, the structure that underlies the detailed information. The science teacher is not only interested in students learning about a particular experiment but also in students learning the idea of scientific experimentation. The social studies teacher wants students not only to create an imaginary culture but also to develop an understanding of culture in general. In the social studies example the 'shape' of information about culture in general was communicated through graphics. The aim was for students to transfer their understanding of the imaginary culture to culture in general. In the history example, the sequence of events was communicated through graphics so that students would attend to the sequence of events in other historical material.

The language teacher wants students to learn the language of a given topic, but also wants students to apply their language learning across the curriculum. The language teacher is not only interested in students learning the language of food classifications or insurance classifications: the wider aim is for students to learn the language of classification in general. In the car insurance example, the 'shape' of classification was communicated through graphics so that students could transfer their language learning to other areas.

To sum up, content teachers and language teachers are both interested in communicating the structure of knowledge as an aid to transfer of learning. The aims of the content teacher relate to the cognitive aspects of the structure of knowledge; the aims of the language teacher relate to the language aspect of the structure of knowledge.

Figure 2.5 presents a framework for the structure of knowledge which teachers can apply to many topics. The framework is not offered as a final and complete pattern, but can be expanded upon by adding other structures of knowledge. It is a focus for discussion and action by people working on the problem of relating language and content, to be expanded and modified as experience dictates.

Practical knowledge versus theoretical knowledge

The main contrast in the organizing framework is between general, theoretical knowledge and specific, practical knowledge. (See Figure 2.5 or the more formal Figure 2.7.) The difference between general and specific knowledge can be illustrated by the difference between classification and description. A classification is a grouping of

Figure 2.7
Formal Statement of Knowledge Framework

ACTIVITY

	Action situation	Background knowledge	
	Practical	Theoretical	
	Particulars–existing at a particular time and place	Universals– timeless	
Description	State of affairs A at T_1*	state of affairs A includes or excludes state of affairs B	Concepts and Classification
Sequence	state A at T_1 is followed by state B at T_2	state A is necessary or sufficient for state B	Principles
Choice	state A and state B are alternative futures at T_1	state A is preferable to state B	Evaluation

*T_{1-n} = different points in time.

concepts, or classes of things and events. A classification groups particular things and events while description describes particular things and events. Essentially, this is the difference between a concept and examples of the concept, between the concept 'fruit' and examples like actual apples, pears or oranges. A concept is a class of items which have a common characteristic; a concept like 'tree' or 'dog' or 'clock' groups together a number of particular things all existing at different times and places, on different occasions—actual trees or dogs or clocks. The concept itself is 'timeless'; it does not exist at any particular time and place. The concept is a universal and its instances are particular.*

Particular things can often be represented by pictures, like a photograph of a particular man or a particular apple. But concepts are usually represented by visual or verbal symbols, a stick figure or a pictograph of a man, or the word 'fruit' or tables and graphs. Specialists in visual aids make a distinction in this way between visuals that are realistic and visuals that are symbolic. Perhaps the best-known discussion of this distinction is the "cone of experience" (Dale, 1954:43). The cone of experience begins with the symbolic and ends with the realistic: it starts with verbal symbols and visual symbols; continues through still pictures to moving pictures to exhibits, to field trips, to demonstrations, to dramatized experiences; and finally ends in direct, purposeful experiences.

Looking at the practical and the theoretical in education generally, we can divide ways of teaching and learning into expository approaches and experiential approaches. Expository approaches, like the use of the lecture, the textbook, and classroom discussion are essentially verbal and explicit. They are particularly appropriate to the symbolic and theoretical aspects of a topic. More appropriate to the practical aspects of a topic are experiential approaches: experience in the laboratory or the workshop, practical activity whether in art, music or home economics, field-trips, first hand contact with data in discovery learning, demonstrations whether live or on film. Role playing and simulation games offer ways of recreating a practical situation, as do case studies. All are experiential in that they are ways of learning through action. All work with specific cases, action situations, examples, data, or performances. However, it is important to remember that there is nothing unintellectual about them; case studies are a favored method of the Harvard Business School.

---

* "We shall find it convenient only to speak of things [i.e. particulars] *existing* when they are in time, that is to say, when we can point to some time *at* which they exist (not excluding the possibility of their existing at all times). Thus, thoughts and feelings, minds and physical objects *exist*. But universals do not exist in this sense; we shall say that they *subsist* or *have being*, where 'being' is opposed to 'existence' as being timeless. The world of universals, therefore, may be described as the world of being. The world of being is unchangeable, rigid, exact, delightful to the mathematician, the logician, the builder of metaphysical systems, and all who love perfection more than life. The world of existence is fleeting, vague, without sharp boundaries, without any clear plan or arrangement, but it contains all thoughts and feelings, all the data of sense, and all physical objects, everything that can do either good or harm, everything that makes any difference to the value of life and the world" (Russell, 1912:99–100).

To sum up, general theoretical knowledge deals with general concepts that are presented through language or through symbolic visuals such as charts, tables, and graphs. It is most easily communicated through expository teaching and learning. On the other hand, specific practical knowledge deals with specific things and events which can be presented through pictures, films, drama, or by direct experience of the things and events themselves. It is most easily communicated through experiential learning and teaching.

2.4 THE CONCEPT OF AN ACTIVITY AS A BASIS FOR THE KNOWLEDGE FRAMEWORK

We began this chapter by discussing topics, but the knowledge framework uses the more helpful notion of an activity. Topic or theme-based teaching comes from an educational tradition that introduced into the curriculum the community activities, endeavors, tasks and occupations that students were familiar with and interested in.

'Activity' is a more precise concept than 'topic'. A topic is anything that can be talked about; an activity is a combination of action and theoretical understanding.

The organizing framework presented in this chapter is based on the concept of an activity. It is a model of the structure of knowledge of an activity. But unfortunately, the term 'activity' has been given many meanings in education, and generally has come to mean something we get students to do. In this discussion the term 'activity' has a less vague meaning. (See also the appendix to Chapter 2.) Consistent with Dearden, we define it not just as action, but as a combination of action and theoretical understanding:

> . . . a human activity is not just, nor indeed necessarily, a movement of the body . . . All human activities, even the most grossly physical, are necessarily mental activities . . . activities necessarily involve consciousness of one's situation apprehended under some description . . . The meaning of what people do, the correct description of their activities, becomes more and more transparent to us as we come to understand a form of social life . . . and the concepts developed by its communities of theoretical inquirers" (Dearden, 1968:132–134).

The two aspects of an activity, action and theoretical understanding, match the two sides of the framework. The specific, practical side we term an action situation, and the general, theoretical side we term background knowledge. Following our framework, an action situation is the specific, practical part or aspect of an activity and includes the knowledge structures of description, sequence, and choice. The background knowledge is the general, theoretical part or aspect of an activity and includes the knowledge structures of classification, principles, and evaluation.

The two aspects of an activity can be illustrated by the game of chess (Figure 2.8). The action situation is analogous to a case study. In chess the action situation would be playing a particular game of chess at a particular time and place. Particular games are

Figure 2.8

ACTIVITY: CHESS

	Action Situation (Practical)	Background Knowledge (Theoretical)	
Description	identify chess pieces	classify chess pieces	Classification
Sequence	sequence moves	understand the rules for moves	Principles
Choice	choose appropriate moves	evaluate moves according to strategies	Evaluation

action situations, and the player must be able to observe (describe) the chess pieces, sequence their moves, and choose between moves with different outcomes. The background knowledge is the general aspect of the activity—the rules and strategies of chess. They are timeless and allow us to understand and interpret an action situation. Consequently, the chess pieces can be classified (rooks, knights, pawns), rules for the movement of different types of chessmen must be known, and strategies can be evaluated as being skillful, cunning, elegant, and so on.

People playing chess make various physical movements which are correctly described only when interpreted through the rules and strategies of chess. The rules of chess contain the concepts of the game and are abstract in the sense that they are not limited to any time or place. Actual occasions of play do occur at a particular time and place with people and boards and chess pieces. But when we see chess played on two different occasions, it is the concepts of the game that enable us to say "same again."

The activity of chess, therefore, is composed of both action situations and background knowledge. Moreover, all activities have a practical and theoretical aspect. Both aspects are important in teaching. Without the practical, students cannot apply what they know; without the theoretical, students cannot understand what they are doing, nor transfer what they know.

The organizing framework of knowledge structures is a guide to the transfer of language and thinking skills across the curriculum, since any content area can be seen as consisting of activities. Figure 2.9 offers a series of activities from mathematics, English literature, computer science, music, science, and social studies. For each activity, it gives an action situation and the background knowledge necessary for the learner to understand and interpret the action situation. Though only one activity has been offered for each content area, it can be shown that each content area can be divided into a series of action situations, each with its necessary background knowledge.

Figure 2.9

ACTIVITY		
Content Area	*Action Situation*	*Background Knowledge*
Chess	playing an actual game	rules and strategies of chess
Algebra	solving the equation $5r^2 + 5 = 130$	rules for symbol manipulation and proof procedures
Computer programming	writing a program	knowledge of the programming language
Literature	appreciating "Hamlet"	dramatic conventions
Science	doing an electrolysis experiment	scientific theory and experimental inquiry
Music	playing a piece of music	music theory and instrumental techniques
Social studies	formulating an opinion on a social issue	research findings and value principles

Together, action situations and background knowledge constitute an activity.

Activity as a central idea in education

The concept of an activity is so central to education that education can be defined in terms of activity. Across the curriculum we find a vast array of activities: designing scientific experiments, composing music, analyzing historical events, interpreting literature, and so on. And, the examples of topics given earlier—insuring and driving a car, buying and preparing food, and even developing a culture in an imaginary society— are all activities. The approach used with them can be used with any activity and applies to education in general. In fact, public activities are the basis for the definition of education given by the philosopher Richard Peters:

> Education, therefore, has to be described as initiation into activities, or modes of thought and conduct [i.e. thought and action] that are worthwhile (Peters, 1966:55).

It is also helpful to see the idea of activities in a historical perspective:

Whether one goes back to the Egyptians, the Babylonians, or even the ancient Chinese, the story is likely to be the same—the curriculum, whether formal or informal, took its origin in the daily activities of the people. Each succeeding generation, in order to become competent to assume the tasks of adults, had a particular curriculum of training to undergo. The would-be artisan had his craft to learn, the warrior skill at arms and the priest his arts and sciences (Brubacher, 1947:250).

The functional origin of the curriculum reminds us of the link between the content of the curriculum and the public activities of society into which the new generation is being initiated.

Activity is a broad integrating idea relevant to all teaching and learning, and it can take a wide variety of forms. Of course, it need not involve physical action. Solving problems in arithmetic is an activity. And a large-scale activity can contain other activities as parts of it, just as many tasks contain subtasks.

Activity versus verbalism: learning and language in context

In less complex societies much is learned informally and incidentally by direct experience. But as societies become more complex the need increases for formal or intentional teaching and learning in educational institutions. This brings with it the danger that formal education will become too isolated from life experience. Formal education will tend towards verbalism, or the mechanical memorization of sentences and undigested information. Dewey relates this tendency to the

> . . . ordinary notion of education: the notion which ignores its social necessity and its identity with all human association that affects conscious life and which identifies it with imparting information about remote matters and the conveying of learning through verbal signs: the acquisition of literacy (Dewey, 1916:8).

Dewey contrasts verbalism with activity. The concept of activity is a corrective to verbalism. In an activity, words and information are integrated with thought and action.

> Words, the counters for ideas, are . . . easily taken for ideas. And in just the degree in which mental activity is separated from active concern with the world, for doing something and connecting the doing with what is undergone, words, symbols, come to take the place of ideas . . . . (ibid.:168).

> Wisdom has never lost its association with the proper direction of life. Only in education, never in the life of the farmer, sailor, merchant, physician, or laboratory experimenter, does knowledge mean primarily a store of information aloof from doing (ibid.:218).

An activity, then, combines theory (background knowledge) and practice (action situations). Learning an activity is learning both theory and practice. Verbal, expository learning is essential for understanding theory and symbolic knowledge, but it needs to be associated with life experience and practical knowledge. Consequently, Dewey recommends that verbal, expository learning should be complemented with practical, experiential learning.

Language teaching tends to concentrate on discourse and ignore its relation to activity. Language is removed from its context of thought and action, sabotaging the goal of teaching communication by eliminating what is to be communicated about. This is part of a larger tendency to verbalism in the tradition of education generally. But verbalism has disadvantages for all students, first and second language learners alike. Students are presented with the final results of knowledge but not with data and experiences to think about. They are presented with talk and writing but not with anything to talk or write about. ESL students are particularly disadvantaged, for verbalism relies on exactly what they lack—a good knowledge of the language of instruction. Giving students more access to practical experience, specifics, data, enables them to use their learning powers and to engage in worthwhile learning processes. *But doing is not an alternative to knowing; it is a way of knowing. And activity is not an alternative to talk; it is a context for talk.*

2.5 SUMMARY AND CONCLUSION

We have introduced a knowledge framework and have shown how the framework applies across the curriculum. We have also indicated how the framework can aid the development of communication, thinking, and language. It can be used to teach themes or topics and to adapt materials for second language learners.

The framework is based on the concept of an activity, and therefore it applies across the curriculum, because the concept of an activity is common to all curricula. All curricula, formal or informal, have as their goal the initiation of the learner into the activities of society. The framework simply picks out the knowledge structures common to all these activities.

In the framework, knowledge is divided into specific, practical knowledge and general, theoretical knowledge. Practical knowledge will include description, sequence, and choice, and theoretical knowledge will include classification, principles, and evaluation. In teaching, practical knowledge is usually communicated through experiential learning and often represented in pictorial graphics. By contrast, theoretical knowledge is usually taught through expository learning and is often represented by symbolic graphics.

The framework has been applied successfully in the classroom. When we integrate language learning with learning an activity, we integrate language learning with subject matter learning. In picking out the knowledge structures common to all activities, the framework provides for transfer of learning from one activity to another. For the content teacher, this means that it can help with the transfer of thinking skills. For the language teacher, this means that it can help with the transfer of language learning.

In the following chapters we will look at the practical and theoretical sides of the framework more closely, pointing out their potential for language development.

APPENDIX

I claim that any activity has the knowledge framework outlined in Figures 2.5 and 2.7. Some supporting evidence can be found in discussions of activities in educational philosophy and of 'lifeworlds' in sociology, although there is by no means common agreement on the knowledge structures of activities.

Dewey makes it clear that an activity contains description, sequence, and choice. The knowledge structure of an activity is reflected in the way an individual directs thought and action toward a goal and creates a pattern of activity:

> . . . the aim as a foreseen end gives direction to the activity . . . . The foresight functions in three ways. In the first place, it involves careful *observation of the given conditions* to see what are the means available for reaching the end, and to discover the hindrances in the way. In the second place, it suggests the proper order or *sequence* in the use of means. It facilitates an economical selection and arrangement. In the third place, it makes the *choice* of alternatives possible. If we can predict the outcome of acting this way or that, we can then compare the value of two courses of action; we can pass judgement upon their relative desirability (Dewey, 1916:102).

Sociological research shows how this knowledge framework appears in the activites or 'lifeworlds' of social groups quite remote from formal education. Letkeman (1973) studied the criminal world of safecrackers. His informants *classified* noncriminals as "squares" or "square johns," and true criminals as "rounders." Within the "criminal" category, "rounders" are contrasted with "bums," who lack the dedication and stability of the true criminal, and "young punks" who lack maturity and seriousness. The process of safecracking is divided into three procedures in *sequence*: "casing" (the process of looking for and assessing a potential job), "making the in" (gaining entry to the place and dealing with locks and burglar alarms) and the act of theft itself (Letkeman 1973:51). Naturally, the safecracker has an expert knowledge of the *principles* of opening safes. As for *evaluation*, the highest value in a crime need not necessarily be money: it may be satisfaction in a job well done:

> What is it in safeblowing that gives you the biggest kick? . . . I guess it's when it goes off . . . . That's the point—did it work? Does it open properly? Did I put in too much or too little? That's the big spot. Someone asked whether the excitement over the door opening was not really a matter of curiosity as to how much money might be in the safe. To this he strongly objected: 'Never! The money is secondary— you take what there is.' (Letkeman, 1973).

The term 'activity' has been used in different ways in the literature, and the resulting confusion makes it difficult to see the value of the idea. The activity model is not simply a way of analyzing a social practice. Nor does it merely mean that the learner should be actively engaged in learning tasks rather than being a passive receiver.

Besides its knowledge framework, an activity has other aspects which are important in learning and teaching. In this book, an activity means a social practice, a form of social life that has a publicly acknowledged structure and standards. However, I believe that there are at least three other perspectives that one can take on an activity, and because the term activity has been used in a variety of different ways in the literature of education, these perspectives should be specified.

When we talk about learning English, we can distinguish among at least: the grammar of English; the psycholinguistic processes of a competent speaker of English; what a learner knows about English; and the learner's learning strategies and processes. These are all considerations when we look at a case of someone learning English. Figure 2.10 categorizes these four perspectives by distinguishing between the expert and the learner, and between the state of knowledge and the process of using or acquiring knowledge.

Figure 2.10

Perspectives on an Activity

	State of Knowledge	Process of Using or Acquiring Knowledge
Expert	a) *Expert Knowledge* the grammar of standard English	b) *Critical Creativity* psycholinguistic processes
Learner	c) *Learner's Knowledge* a grammar of a child's language	d) *Learning and Development* the process and strategies of language acquisition

Learning English can then be seen from the four perspectives in Figure 2.10. The grammar of English (a) is what the ideal competent speaker knows. How a competent speaker of English uses this knowledge requires us to look at the psycholinguistic processes of the speaker (b). What the learner knows about English requires an analysis of a stage of learning, such as a grammar of a child's language (c). And how the learner learns English demands an account of learning strategies and processes (d). These four perspectives we can term expert knowledge, critical creativity, learner's knowledge, and learning and development.

Although in this book I have taken the expert knowledge or public concept perspective and defined the knowledge structures within it, all activities can be viewed from one or all four of the perspectives. Consider chess as an example. In Figure 2.11 we can distinguish between: what the ideal competent player knows; how the expert player operates with this knowledge; what a learner of chess knows; and the learner's strategies and processes for learning chess.

Figure 2.11

Perspectives on the Activity of Chess

	State of Knowledge	Process of Using or Acquiring Knowledge
Expert	a) *Expert Knowledge* the rules of chess	b) *Critical Creativity* expert chess playing
Learner	c) *Learner's Knowledge* a beginner's understanding of chess	d) *Learning and Development* processes and strategies of learning chess

Summarizing, we have:

1. *The public concept (expert knowledge)*. This is the collective, public aspect of an activity. A social activity as a form of social life has a publicly acknowledged structure and standards.

2. *Critical creativity*. This is the individual and mental aspect of an activity, the thought process of an expert engaged in the activity. This includes not only rule-governed creativity but also a critical perspective based on the aims, standards, and strategies of the activity.

3. *The learner's concept*. This is the learner's understanding of an activity, the state of the learner's knowledge.

4. *Learning and development*. The educational aspect of an activity is the process that takes a learner from a beginner's understanding to an expert's understanding. It includes the processes of learning and teaching that lead to competence in the activity.

Though the expert knowledge or public concept perspective is emphasized here, the other perspectives should not be forgotten, because they too are important in any case of learning.

EXERCISES FOR CHAPTER TWO

1. Examine an example of theme-based language teaching material. Use the references in the suggested readings for this chapter as a guide; for example, Sampson and Lynsky. Discuss how the material provides for communication, the development of language, and the development of thinking.

2. Identify a few activities in any subject area of physics, literature, history, geography, etc. Use Figure 2.9 as a guide. For each activity, give an example of an action situation and list some of the background knowledge required.

3. Analyze an activity into its parts. Pick any activity of interest to you. Using the car

insurance material as an example, fill out the chart of knowledge structures in Chapter 2. Look for one case of each knowledge structure. You may find it easiest to think first of a process or series of actions in the activity as an action strip or a film. This can then be broken down into description (of a single frame), sequence (a series of frames), and alternatives or choice points (alternative possibilities). Then consider the background knowledge that is required and look for cases of concepts and classification, principles, and goals and values. Think of what the participant or spectator needs to know in order to make sense of the activity and interpret it correctly. Examples of activities include: using the library, designing a research project, renting an apartment, applying for a bank loan, participation in a case in the law courts, dong school science experiments, surveying a community, playing a game in physical education, solving mathematical problems, and programming a computer.

4. Find public education material and adapt it for the second language learner. Librarians can be very helpful in locating sources. Consider all types of social agencies, marketing boards and government departments, e.g., those concerned with public health, safety, nutrition, child care, etc.

5. Find a subject matter lesson or unit and adapt it for second language learners. In what ways would second language learners find the material difficult? What parts of the material would they find easy? How could the material be adapted and used so that second language students could understand it? How could it be used to help the student become a more independent learner of this content area?

6. Review a content textbook, looking particularly at the graphics it includes. What seem to be the typical and natural graphics in this content area? How do they relate to the content material? Do they reveal general patterns of organization in the content area? (e.g., pictures of famous people could indicate a biographical organization, maps could indicate an organization around places.)

7. Review a second language textbook, looking at the graphics it includes. How are they used by the textbook? How are students expected to use them? How do the graphics relate to the language being developed? Are the graphics similar to or different from the graphics in content textbooks?

8. Some audiovisual specialists make a distinction between realistic, pictorial graphics, like photographs, and symbolic graphics, like a statistical frequency distribution. A picture story is realistic, while a classification tree is symbolic. (N.B. The distinction between realistic and symbolic is not always clear-out and may be a matter of degree.) Make a list of realistic, pictorial types of graphics and a list of symbolic, non-pictorial types. Collect some examples. What kinds of material contain mainly pictorial graphics?

   What kinds of material contain mainly symbolic graphics? Is there a difference between the kind of information conveyed by each type of graphic (e.g., specific information vs. general information)?

9. Look at the chart of knowledge structures. Compare and contrast it with similar ideas in any educational psychology textbook you are familiar with. For example, Gagne (1970) mentions the teaching of concepts and principles. A major difference is one of emphasis: here we are interested in identifying concepts and principles as they occur in resource material and in topic information. Educational psychologists are more concerned with the teaching and learning of concepts and principles. How far do you find their suggestions for teaching and learning helpful? How do they relate to your own work?

10. Learners find it difficult to express what they mean in a second language. Giving them a chart to fill in is one way of making their task easier and smoothing the transition to independent communication. List a number of ways in which the teacher can arrange support to help learners express themselves. Expand on the following ideas:

Language: consider guiding questions, statements with blanks, sentences in scrambled order.

Graphics: consider pointing, partly completed pictures and charts, forms and tables to be filled in, sets of pictures to be arranged in order, models to assemble.

People: Groups of students can often pool their resources to express ideas more effectively. Consider pair work and group work. Also consider the language experience approach where the teacher guides students in expressing their thoughts.

CHAPTER TWO
SUGGESTED READINGS

Allen, J.P. and J. Howard. 1981. "Subject-related ESL: an Experiment in Communicative Language Teaching." *Canadian Modern Language Review*, 37:535–550. Illustrates a subject-related approach to materials design in order to infuse educationally worthwhile content into the ESL class. Establishes specific links between language practice and school subjects.

Brubacher, J. 1947. *A History of the Problems of Education.* New York: McGraw Hill. A history of education which discusses John Dewey's ideas and places them in a historical context.

Candlin, C. and C. Edelhoff. 1982. *Challenges: Teacher's Guide.* London: Longman. Presents a theme-based language course and explains the principles that guided its design.

Dale, E. 1954. *Audiovisual Methods in Teaching.* New York: Holt Rinehart. Part 1 discusses the theory of audiovisual instruction in relation to experience and communication.

Dearden, R. 1968. *The Philosophy of Primary Education.* London: Routledge and Kegan Paul. Discusses activity in relation to main aspects of curriculum and different forms of knowledge.

Dewey, J. 1916. *Democracy and Education.* New York: Macmillan. Dewey's chief work on education.

Dworkin, M. 1959. *Dewey on Education.* New York: Columbia University. Contains Dewey's early writings on education.

Frankena, W. 1965. *Three Historical Philosophies of Education.* Chicago: Scott Foresman. Gives a clear account of Dewey's philosophy of education and the role of activities within it.

Garvie, E. 1976. *Breakthrough to Fluency.* Oxford: Blackwell. A practical approach to teaching English as a second language to young children of 5 + years, and a thoughtful general perspective. Chapter 8, "The Centre of Interest: an Integration of Learning" shows how the teaching of a theme can link experience, thought, and language.

Goffman, E. 1974. *Frame Analysis.* New York: Harper and Row. A sociological analysis of the way situations are defined, with the organizational principles that seem to underlie these definitions. Basic terms are the 'strip' of experience, that is, sequence of happenings in the stream of ongoing activity, and the 'frame,' the principles of organization which govern the interpretation of events.

Levine, J. H. Hester, and G. Skirrow. 1972. *Scope Stage 2.* London: Longman. A language development course for use in multiracial classes with children aged 8 to 13. The materials are based on the study of three themes: homes, water, and travel.

Lynskey, A. 1974. *Children and Themes*. Oxford:Oxford University Press. A handbook designed to help first language teachers who are seeking to widen the experience of young children by a thematic approach through drama and literature.

Peters, R.S. 1966. *Ethics and Education*. London:Allen and Unwin. Chapter 5 discusses education as the initiation of others into worthwhile activities from a philosopher's standpoint.

Sampson, G. 1977. "A Real Challenge to ESL Methodology." *TESOL Quarterly 11*, 3:241–256. Argues that ESL practices should be based on principles common to approaches underlying both first and second language teaching. Discusses theme-based teaching.

Wright, A. 1976. *Visual Materials for the Language Teacher*. London:Longman. A practical handbook for language teachers which gives an analysis of visual materials in language teaching.

Chapter 3

Language and
Action Situations

3.1 INTRODUCTION

Central to the knowledge framework discussed in the last chapter is the recommendation that a framework for teaching be based on an activity. This framework offers a rich potential for teachers, because the concept of an activity applies across the curriculum, and the framework guides the transfer of thinking skills and language skills across content areas.

In that chapter we divided an activity into its specific, practical aspect and its general theoretical aspect. (See Figures 2.5 and 2.9.) The specific, practical aspect is an action situation, such as a particular game of chess played at a particular time and place. The general, theoretical aspect is background knowledge, such as the rules and strategies of chess, which are timeless. A whole activity then, like chess, includes both aspects. This chapter will explore the practical side of an activity, the action situation. The theoretical side of an activity, background knowledge, will be developed in the following chapter.

The organizing framework shows that the practical aspect of an activity, the action situation, contains description, sequence and choice. For each particular game of chess, the player to must be able to recognize (describe) the individual chessmen, sequence moves and choose well among the possible moves. Similarly, in the photostory (Figure 2.2), the learners need to be able to recognize items shown in the story (insurance offices, claims centers), to understand sequences shown (procedures for reporting an accident), and be aware of the reasons behind choices shown (actions to take when an accident occurs). A competent participant in an action situation can recognize relevant items, persons, and scenes, can carry out suitable procedures, and can make informed choices. All action situations, not only these two examples of a game of chess or an auto accident, contain description, sequence, and choice. This pattern is a key to communication, thinking, and language in action situations.

By developing the language resources necessary to talk about description, sequence, and choice, we have an opportunity to develop a broad competence in the language which is transferable to the learner's needs across content areas. Therefore we must look at how description, sequence and choice in action situations can be used in the classroom and list language items (such as grammatical rules, semantic notions, and speech acts) which can guide the work of the language teacher. We will also describe the limitations that have been placed on the development of action situations for language teaching by current practices and views, and look at what avenues are open to develop more transferable language learning.

Action situations are often shown in ESL classrooms by action strips. I have argued here and elsewhere that although graphics are used extensively in teaching language, they offer a far greater opportunity for language learning than their current use would suggest. Consequently this chapter will also outline the use of flowcharts, usually associated with computers, for showing action situations. They are not necessarily a preferred way to communicate about action situations, but they are of use to the language learner and teacher since they clearly show description, sequence, and choice in action situations, and they have been used successfully by my own students in their classrooms.

Finally, we must recognize that the basis for our teaching in the classroom is not restricted to educational theory. For those with an interest in the broader context of action situations, we can show how the distinctions we make when looking at the specific, practical aspect of an activity fit into a broader general theory of action offered by the work of philosophers.

But first, how are action situations currently viewed from the standpoint of the language teacher in his or her classroom?

3.2 ACTION SITUATIONS AND LANGUAGE LEARNING

There is wide agreement that young children learn their first language through action situations. The speech of young learners and of those speaking to them is oriented to action in the here-and-now (Newport et al., 1977). It is therefore recommended that second language learners learn in a similar fashion (Dulay, Burt and Krashen, 1982). And, in fact, second language learners are often placed in art, music, and physical education classes which offer learning opportunities in action situations. They also learn in action situations in their mathematics classes where they perform calculations and solve equations i.e., perform actions on symbols.

Experience seems to support the belief that students learn both subject matter and language in these subject areas, although it is not easy to find relevant research evidence. It seems likely that students will learn the language which is special to these subjects. An important question, however, is whether it is possible for students to advance in wider language development in these circumstances. In other words, can action situations provide for progressive and systematic language development?

In the past, language teaching has often failed to develop the language learning potential of action situations. Action situations have not been explored in any depth, and at the same time beginning learners have been presented with language removed from any context of action. It has been assumed that language in action situations is limited to the here-and-now and special to the particular situation.

One reason for this failure is a limited view of action situations. Action in situations can be seen in at least three ways: as conditioned responses, as conventional behavior, or as decision-making. Each view has different implications for language learning.

Wilkins (1976:164) outlines a conditioned response view when he describes situational language teaching. First, he suggests, the action situation is the objectively describable physical setting. Second, he suggests there is a one-way causal relation between this setting and talk: the setting causes the talk and the speaker is at the mercy of the setting. Third, the speaker is limited by the setting to a restricted selection of the language which is predictable by the outside observer. Following this approach the learner in an action situation is merely a learner of stock verbal responses.

In the conventional behavior view, a person in an action situation is regarded as following rules of language and of social behavior appropriate to the situation. Language learning in action situations is then seen merely as a matter of learning language rules and rules of appropriateness. For example, the learner might be learning the appropriate conventions for polite requests. Many language courses follow this approach.

For understanding a decision-making view, consider the meaning of 'situation' to an existentialist philosopher like Sartre:

> Mountain-climbing, I find myself at the edge of an abyss, suddenly afraid of falling to my death. But because I am afraid, because I internalise the situation as revealed by fear, I begin by moving more carefully, watching my steps. As I do, the world becomes transformed into a set of possibilities I control through choice and action. These possibilities . . . . . . constitute what Sartre speaks of as my situation, of which I am the source. Sartre means by situation an active structuring of the world from the perspective of an engaged consciousness . . . . (Danto, 1975:75).

Human choice is central to action situations. As we will see, it is central even to the very simple situations we will discuss. Talk about choice is talk which goes beyond the limits of the immediate situation and calls for a wider language potential. From the decision-making view, a person in an action situation is making reasoned choices about what to say and what to do. Language learning in action situations is therefore more than learning to speak appropriately. It includes talking about and learning about reasons for acting. This book takes the decision-making view of action situations.

With these views in mind we now consider the teaching of language in action situations, starting with dialogues.

3.3 ACTION SITUATIONS
AND DIALOGUES

Most oral language courses will contain language in action situations. As yet, a major, and unresolved, problem with the courses is how learning about language can be organized in concert with learning about situations. In many of these courses, in addition to teaching language we are trying to teach situational information as well. The unresolved problem, therefore, is how to respond to the students' need to speak and act in the target community. Usually, however, this difficult problem is avoided by attending to the language only and ignoring the action situation. This reduces language in action situations to dialogues, to which we will now turn.

The idea of the dialogue is very familiar to language teachers, but it is worth repeating some of the points about dialogue as it was seen within the audiolingual tradition. "The short dialogue is frequently used as one of the steps leading from imitative repetition toward free conversation . . . . A dialogue is any oral interchange between two or more people . . . . It may limit itself to one new grammar problem embedded in known vocabulary, or to new vocabulary in known grammatical structures" (McCready, 1972). It should be memorizable and have a language teaching point. Its role is to teach the language while maintaining the interest of the students and having some credibility as a sample of talk. Student activities include memorizing the dialogue and using it for substitution drills. In sum, the dialogue is seen only as an instance of the vocabulary items and grammatical structures of the language. This is decontextualized dialogue.

More recent developments of conversational interchange include the use of dialogues recorded in situations where the learners anticipate they will interact, and the use of situational role plays which enable learners to practice conversational interaction. Clearly the context of the dialogue is of importance. The learners may discuss information on the background of the dialogue: for example, in a banking situation, they may discuss how to open an account. Assessing the effectiveness of the role play raises issues well beyond questions of linguistic correctness. When opening an account, do the speakers appear to know the appropriate procedures? This is contextualized dialogue. Dialogue is now seen as part of effective (or ineffective) action in a situation which requires contextual knowledge. It is not enough to see dialogue as "any oral interchange": we distinguish between effective and ineffective, knowledgeable and ill-founded dialogue by relating dialogue to the action situation.

With decontextualized dialogue, the target for the learner is the conversationalist. Dialogue is seen as general conversation between "talking heads." Analysis of the dialogue requires analysis of talk only. However, with contextualized dialogue, the target for the learner is the effectively communicating agent. Talk is seen as an integral part of an activity such as setting up an account. Analysis of the contextualized dialogue then requires the analysis of talk in relation to activity.

3.4 ACTION SITUATIONS AND COMMUNICATIVE ENVIRONMENTS

An interest in contextualized dialogue demands knowledge of the communicative environment of the learner. We need to know who communicates with the learner and in what situations.

Laird (1977) describes an approach for surveying the communicative environment of the workplace, and part of the survey examines the communication network of the individual. For example, a worker may communicate with her fellow worker, her supervisor, and her shop steward, to name just part of the network. The network is a clue to typical dialogues.

In addition to the communication network of the individual, we need to know about the workplace environment that gives rise to the dialogues within it. Laird suggests gathering information on the daily timetable of the worker, e.g.,

1:10 p.m. A problem with the machine.

Needs to fetch supervisor to report it.

The fitter comes.

Tells the fitter what is wrong.

This puts the dialogue in relation to an action situation of machine breakdown. The worker talks to the supervisor in order to report a machine breakdown and to the fitter in order to have it repaired.

Another part of the survey includes interviews with management and unions about specific problem areas of communication. The interviews revealed the following problems with machine breakdown reports:

(a) need for operatives to improve their level of job-related language. At present all faults have to be corrected by constant badgering and repeated demon- stration.

(b) need to understand procedures for reporting machine breakdowns.

(c) only know the basic principles of the machine and therefore cannot locate point of breakdown (Laird, 1977:17).

The first problem, (a), indicates that workers lack the language to be effective in dialogue. Problems (b) and (c) indicate difficulties in understanding the context of the dialogue: (b) is a problem with the procedures that underlie the dialogue, and (c) is a problem with background knowledge. In an actual interaction about machine break- down, the three are interlinked, and failure could be due to a lack of language, not knowing how to follow the procedure, or not knowing the principles of the machine. To communicate effectively, the worker needs knowledge of both dialogue and action situation.

This type of survey of the communicative environment, then, collects data about both dialogues and action situations. And learners need a knowledge of both if they are to communicate effectively.

But there is a problem here. It has been customary for language and content to be taught separately. Either language is taught or information is taught, but it is not clear how to attend to both systematically. Yet the example of the machine breakdown interaction shows how both are naturally and logically related in actual communication. The issue then is to show how language teaching can take advantage of this natural relationship, to show how to teach situational language and situational information at the same time.

3.5 ACTION SITUATIONS
AND GRAPHICS

Graphics can be used to teach situational language and situational information at the same time. Recall again the car insurance photostory. The photostory presented dialogue in an action situation. The situational information was shown by the pictures. This can be done for any dialogue and any action situation.

How is situational information shown by graphics? It is only necessary to consider the many everyday examples where an action situation is represented by a visual. Think of basic instructional manuals for everyday machines like dishwashers or cars. A dishwashing manual, for instance, may show a multi-step procedure for operating the dishwasher. Each step is illustrated by a drawing (Step 1—Prepare Your Dishes), and the whole sequence is an action strip. Examples could be multiplied indefinitely. If I want to cut down a tree, a series of pictures shows me a way of doing it so the tree does not fall on top of me. In brief, simple processes and procedures are commonly shown by a sequence of pictures in an action strip. Each picture of an action strip is a selective description of some state of affairs—a hand pouring detergent, the layout of an electrical circuit, the ingredients of a recipe. If situational information can be described by a picture or a diagram, it can be represented in a frame of a strip.

Language teachers have long used action strips to show dialogues. If we have a talking heads conversation, each frame can have a talking head with its remark written in a bubble. If we want to include something of the backdrop of the conversation, it can be drawn in the frame. Newspapers contain many examples. Learners may work with the dialogue, describe the state of affairs in a frame, or narrate the sequence of action. To sum up, an action strip can combine situational language and situational content and can be developed as dialogue, description, and narration.

A limitation of the strip is that it is not easy to show alternatives and the reasons for choosing between them. Yet choice is an important element in action situations.

Showing alternatives by themselves is simple. One example from a third world family planning program consists of two pictures, each showing a family. The first family looks hungry, is poorly dressed, and has many children. The second looks well-fed and well-dressed and has just two children. Another pair of pictures from the *Scope Senior Course* (Davies and Hadi, 1973) shows one job applicant at an employment interview greeting the secretary pleasantly and another job applicant bursting into her office and shocking her out of her wits. Alternatives like this are often used as a basis for group discussion. By contrast, inserting alternatives into cartoon strips and showing the reasons for choosing between them is less familiar.

A device which does show choices and their reasons and which outlines more complex processes in action situations is the flowchart. An example of a flowchart for shopping is given in Figure 3.1. Action strips can be regarded as simple parts of

Figure 3.1
Flowchart of Shopping Situation

C=clerk   S=shopper

Boxes are numbered 1-13

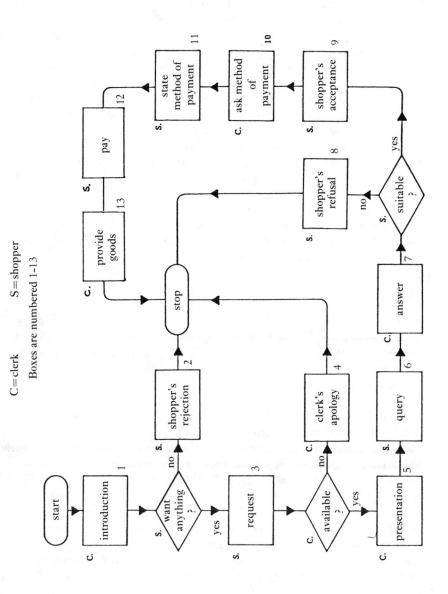

flowcharts. For instance, an action strip of someone shopping could be converted into a very simple flowchart. Each picture of the cartoon strip becomes a box in the flowchart. The usual, more complex flowchart is rather like several related cartoon strips connected up with each other. Perhaps one strip shows the shopper just browsing and refusing the clerk's help, and another strip shows the shopper with something definite in mind, accepting the clerk's help and making a request. Both of these are represented in the first four boxes of the shopping flowchart. Conventionally, the decision to choose between two lines of action is shown by a diamond which states a basis for choosing between them, for instance, whether the shopper has something definite in mind or not. The flowchart therefore contains the equivalent of single pictures (description), strips of pictures (sequence), and choice of pictures (choice).

The flowchart should be able to do whatever the cartoon strip can do, and more. This suggests two tasks. Firstly, since a cartoon strip can present situational language and situational content in combination, so can the flowchart, but with more adequacy. In what follows I will show how this works out. Secondly, since a cartoon strip can be developed as narrative and description, the flowchart should offer both of these plus the discussion of choices. In fact, to put the matter more generally, the elements of the flowchart can lend themselves to the development of the trio familiar to teachers of composition: description, narration, and discussion or argument.

Flowcharts

While the flowchart is usually associated with computers, the best way to get a sense of its scope for representing problem-solving action procedures is to look into the growing literature on algorithms, that is, problem-solving procedures which are effective, easy to use, and communicable by flowchart. Some representative texts are Landa's *Algorithmisation in Learning and Instruction* (Landa, 1974), Lewis, Horabin, and Gan's pamphlet *Flowcharts, Logical Trees and Algorithms for Rules and Regulations* (Lewis et al, 1967), *How to Do Things with Rules* by the lawyers Twining and Miers (Twining and Miers, 1976) and *The Algorithm Writer's Guide* (Wheatley and Unwin, 1972). Much of the work in this field has been done by those interested in applied psychology and instruction, but is not yet well known to language teachers. The topics covered range from mathematical problem solving and official rules and regulations to industrial and commercial applications. The latter are of particular interest because they provide numerous examples of flowcharts oriented to concrete action: getting a central heating system or a car engine to work, the chemical maintenance of feedwater to boilers, diagnosing faults in an electric typewriter. There are likely to be many more in the future. One researcher, Brian Lewis, looking at industrial companies reporting poor performances of certain categories of staff, discovered time and again that "poor performance among workers" was due almost entirely to the fact that nobody had taken the trouble to tell them, in sufficiently clear terms, how to perform their duties correctly. The established literature analyzing mainly nonverbal tasks can be connected with our analysis of purposeful talk through the device of the flowchart.

Flowcharts and dialogues*

With minor modifications of the computer flowchart, the flowchart can help us to outline a speech event or situation so that it can be seen as a whole, while, at the same time, each particular speech act can be isolated and worked on. A flowchart can be used as a map of a transactional relationship between two people, which starts at the first move, providing alternatives to what happens next as it proceeds to the end of the encounter. Each move towards the end is a speech act or a nonverbal act, or both together. At any point along the way, input can be provided by teacher or student. What is important is that the flowchart, prepared by the teacher, should be simple so that it can easily be seen as a bare outline of the situation, with the beginning and the end clearly in view.

Figure 3.1 shows a flowchart that outlines a shopping situation in terms of speech acts. The whole chart covers four possible conversational sequences, for there are just four ways to get to STOP, each one longer than the last. A diamond represents a silent decision made by either the shopper or the clerk, and a box represents at least one speech act or nonverbal act by a participant. Since the actual utterance chosen can vary quite widely, this allows students to suggest suitable utterances of their own choosing. The boxes have been numbered for easy reference.

Beginners could be expected to stay with the basic linguistic exchanges involved in making a purchase. Therefore, flowcharts for this level could be prepared with as few boxes as are necessary for a single lesson. None need contain as many as in this example. Rank beginners would not need more than one sequence prepared by the teacher, and advanced students could suggest additions to an equally simple basic flowchart. For instance, a shopper could discover a flaw in the garment and ask for a reduction in price, or enquire about the possibilities for exchange. The details of the flowchart can be determined by the interests of the students.

With the speech acts so divided, the teacher can prompt students into providing a variety of responses. In a multilevel class, the more advanced students can be expected to provide the responses, which are then repeated by the teacher and the beginning students respectively. In a completely low-level class, pictures or stick figures could be the focus of attention. The following sequences exemplify the sort of role played by the teacher.

(Please refer to the numbered boxes on the flowchart.)

• Teacher Prompts

Shopper's Rejection Sequence:

Box 1.   How does the clerk greet the shopper?

Box 2.   How does the shopper refuse help/say no?

---

* This section is based on work done in collaboration with Naomi Katz. See Mohan and Katz (1977).

Clerk's Apology Sequence:

Box 1. How does the clerk greet the shopper?

Box 3. The shopper asks for a coat/saw some coats advertised.

Box 4. They're all sold out.

- Possible Exchanges Between Clerk and Customer

Rejection Sequence:

Box 1. May I help you?

Box 2. Just looking, thanks.

Apology Sequence:

Box 1. May I help you?

Box 3. Where are the coats that were advertised?

Box 4. I'm sorry but they're all sold out.

Other possibilities include considering ways to show speech act variations of greetings and farewells, opening and closing conversations, indirect forms of requests (*Could you show me*), politeness and rudeness. Since the incident need not flow smoothly, it is possible to explore attention-getters (*Excuse me*), mishearing (*I beg your pardon*), corrections (*These shirts are blue, not white*), and checking back (*Did you say 'blue'?*), to name a few.

Note that these are possible exchanges only. There is a lot of free choice in what can be said at any particular point.

The flow diagram can be enlarged in various ways. Some of the additions we have made can be gathered from the following prompts:

Clerk's Suggestions Segment:

Clerk wants to know the style/the size wanted.

Shopper is not sure of the style/size wanted.

Clerk makes a suggestion.

Shopper's Reservations/Clerk's Substitution Segment:

Clerk shows the shopper a coat.

Shopper is not sure if she likes it. (Shopper's Reservations)

Clerk shows her another one. (Clerk's Subsitution)

Shopper is still not sure if she likes it. (Shopper's Reservations)

Clerk shows her yet another one. (Clerk's Substitution)

Both of these possibilities allow multiple repeats. This can be handled by looping back through the same boxes again and again. In this way, complex dialogues can be produced. Referring back to the flowchart, the *Suggestions* segment would increase the possibilities at box 3, and the *Reservations* segment would increase the possibilities at box 5.

The flowchart is therefore a very useful method of drawing attention to the structure of a situation. Since situations are a source of language problems for the student, the flowchart describes a problem solving strategy for a specific situation which the student can use.

Initially, we introduced the flowchart as a technique for working with the dialogue, and we have shown how a flowchart can represent a whole family of dialogues relating to the same situation. However, the dialogues themselves should be considered as neither set nor enduring, nor the be-all and end-all of the lesson, but simply as a focus for some of the possibilities of the situation at hand.

The flowchart does not represent a limited, restricted, and predictable set of moves. It is rather a bare outline showing the potential for creating further situational possibilities and further language development. It is not a prophecy, but a guide.

There are some more general points to be made about the representation of situations by flowcharts. A situation contains a series of actions which may be verbal, nonverbal, or a blend of the two. It has already been shown how a flowchart can represent a family of dialogues, i.e., a series of verbal actions. And of course a flowchart can show a series of nonverbal actions. This is obvious enough. A flowchart can represent any procedure, whether it be dressing a wound, using a public telephone, mending an electrical fuse, or performing a mathematical calculation. Finally, a flowchart can also show a mixed sequence of verbal and nonverbal actions. The one given here in Figure 3.1 is a case in point. It includes actions like payment and transfer of goods, highly important nonverbal actions (you can be jailed for nonpayment!) and in addition, it puts them in the proper relation to the verbal action. You discuss what you want and then buy it, rather than the other way around.

The most serious limitation of flowcharts is that they represent choice very simply and crudely. They show where choices must be made, but they do not show all of the considerations that enter into a serious choice or decision. Anyone who wishes to represent the detailed structure of a decision situation should consult the literature that analyzes decision making. For instance, an analysis of decision making in business and commerce is given in The *Analysis of Decisions*, Moore and Thomas (1976). We should regard a choice in a flowchart not as automatic, but as a potential starting point for discussion and analysis.

To sum up, the flow diagram is a simple link between the structure of dialogue and the structure of nonverbal action. In effect it acts as a logical skeleton in which actions, verbal or nonverbal, can be explored. Students can develop their understanding of conversational dialogue while developing their understanding of action situations and the choices they contain.

3.6 DISCOURSE ABOUT
ACTION SITUATIONS

We have said that many situational language courses aim only to teach situational dialogues. They do not aim to develop the students' ability to talk about situations. This limits the student, both as a learner of language and as a learner of content.

Action strips and flowcharts present information to be learned about a situation and provide for talk about the action situation. A single picture can be described, a strip or sequence of pictures can be narrated, and a choice between two pictures can be argued over. Similarly, for the flowchart the state of affairs at any box can be described, any path taken by a sequence of action through the flowchart can be narrated, and any decision made at a diamond can be argued over.

When students learn to talk about situations, they can develop the language of description, sequence, and choice. This helps their language development in general. Thus, although the language learned in a situational dialogue may be limited to that particular situation, the language of description, sequence, and choice applies to all situations.

To illustrate this we take an example situation of shopping for food represented by a brief situational dialogue extracted from the flowchart. From this example we can show possibilities for talk about description, sequence, and choice, and list language items appropriate for each. In this way it is possible to see how talk about a situation can be explored for its language learning potential.

Example: shopping for food

> Shopper: Can I see some Camembert cheese, please.
>
> Clerk: Here you are. (*Shows cheese to shopper*)
>
> Shopper: (*Decides on choice*)
>
> > Thank you, I'll take a pound. (*pays*)
> >
> > No, thanks, I'll get something else.

This situation contains actions (*e.g.*, *Shows cheese to shopper*) and other nonverbal elements which can be described, a sequence of action which can be narrated and analyzed, and a decision (*Decides on choice*), which leads to alternative actions (*either/or*) and which can be discussed. It fits into the flowchart in Figure 3.1. Like any situation, it lends itself to the language opportunities which now follow.

Description

Basis: a typical situation includes participants, actions, objects, and a scene or setting. Dramatization or pictures show these visually. All can be described by the teacher.

Examples: shopper gives an identifying description of the item wanted. Shopper and clerk compare and contrast items.

Classroom activity: learners role play shopper and clerk using labels, advertisements, and catalogue descriptions of goods for information. More generally, a description of the state of affairs at any point in the situation gives a starter for role playing the remainder of the situation.

Grammar: NP +BE +NP/Adj./Prep. Phrase; there +BE +NP; relative clauses, reduced relative clauses, adjectives, demonstratives, articles; NP +HAVE +NP, possessive pronouns, genitives; spatial prepositions; comparative sentences; the same as, different from, and . . . too, but.

Semantic notions: existence, attribution and predication, possession, spatial relations, comparison and contrast.

Speech acts: reference, predication.

Sequence

Basis: A typical situation is a series of related events and actions on a time line. If there is no discourse, we have a chain of actions. With discourse we have a script. These events and actions can be narrated by the teacher.

Example: the clerk's attention is distracted, and the shopper leaves with the goods, mistakenly thinking that they are paid for. The clerk calls the shopper back and they clear up the mistake, establishing the chronological order of events and the reasons for the confusion.

Classroom activity: an extension of the above. Shopper is to be accused of shoplifting. Students create the events which led up to this. Then some take the roles of shopper, clerk, and floorwalker and the rest act as the supervisor and interview the others about what happened. A report on the incident is written combining the interview information. Simpler activities include narrating the script or action chain and issuing instructions to the shopper or clerk.

Grammar: prepositions and prepositional phrases of time, cause, and purpose (at, before, because of); adjuncts of time 'when', and time duration (today, afterwards, since); clauses of time, condition, reason or cause, circumstance, purpose, result; sentence time relaters (first, rest, earlier, later), tenses; quotation, reported speech; imperatives.

Semantic notions: time relations between events; conditions, cause and reason; relation of events to present time of speaking.

Speech acts: report, instruction, explanation (in the sense of identifying antecedents or intended consequences).

Choice

Basis: A typical situation will include intentional actions. Any such action springs from a choice which derives from a decision situation (some choices, of course, are more trivial than others). The decision situation can be stated by the teacher.

Example: the shopper makes a decision to buy or not to buy. This can be by internal deliberation or by discussion. A possible choice can be offered by a proposal and can be rejected with a refutation. Alternatives can be compared and contrasted and their consequences explored.

Classroom activity: the main decision is whether to buy or not. The students create the decision situation that this springs from. This can be simpler or more complex, depending on the level of the students. A statement of a decision situation is the basis for a problem-solving activity. It is worthwhile to review some decision situation elements:

1. Problem-statement of the relevant aspects of the situation.

2. Alternative courses of action and their consequences.

3. A decision on the basis of reasons.

Grammar:

Problem—What *should* I do?

Alternatives—I *can* do *either* X *or* Y.

Reasons—I *must/ought* to/*need* to/do Y.

Decision—I *will* do Y.

The main grammar items here are modals. Mention should be made of related constructions such as *it is possible/necessary to do X*.

Semantic notions: ability, obligation, permission, necessity, possibility, probability, alternation, intention.

Speech acts: appraisals, verdicts, proposals, refutations, advice, recommendations, predictions.

This example action situation shows how talking and learning about any action situation calls for talk about description, sequence, and choice.

Many further ways to develop this talk can be extracted from current language teaching materials. Each of the classroom activities in our shopping example suggests this. Description relates to ways of characterizing people, places, and things, and reporting observations. Sequence is developed in instructions, procedures, stories, and in more complex forms of narration. Choice and decision making is involved in problem solving materials familiar in ESL teaching (see Kettering, 1975), in values clarification techniques (see Howe and Howe, 1975) and in problem posing approaches (see Wallerstein, 1983).

In our example we also listed language items used in English to express the meanings associated with description, sequence, and choice. Many more items can be found in semantic grammars. A good source is Leech and Svartvik (1975) which organizes the items of the language according to the meanings they express. It will be recognized that description, sequence, and choice are made up of a number of fundamental meaning relations: as an example, sequence covers time relations between events. For those seeking time language items to note in the classroom, Leech and Svartvik (1975:63–82) describe in detail how time is expressed in English.

To summarize, the language potential of action situations has often been overlooked because the language of action has been thought to be limited and particular to that situation. This has meant that language teaching has failed to develop the language learning possibilities of action situations. While some of the language of an action situation is likely to be special to that particular situation, the language of description, sequence, and choice is not. The ability to describe, narrate, and discuss is part of communication development in general.

3.7 TEACHING SITUATIONAL INFORMATION

Sometimes situational language courses do teach information about action situations, but this is usually viewed as an alternative to teaching language. It is not. On the contrary, teaching and learning about a situation is an avenue to develop the students' ability to talk about situations. This can be seen clearly if situational content objectives are organized under description, sequence, and choice, as many already are. The content material then lends itself to language development.

The teacher preparing to teach about an action situation will find that many content objectives are organized this way. In the case of shopping, the shopper needs (i) to be able to identify and describe goods, (ii) to understand procedures for payment, (iii) to weigh considerations of what goods to choose. Accordingly, in *English for Adult Living* (Blosser, 1979), a competency based ESL survival skills course, situational information is organized under situational objectives like (i) identifying foods, (ii) handling currency and making correct change, (iii) choosing the best food bargain in terms of price, quality, and quantity by comparative shopping. More generally, content objectives can be related to the flowchart. Wherever objects are mentioned in the flowchart, the learner may have to identify and discriminate between them. Wherever there are processes incorporated in the flowchart, the learner may have to understand their sequence. Wherever there is choice, the learner may have to gain insight into the relevant considerations.

The thinking skills that relate to description, sequence and choice apply to all action situations. And lists of these thinking skills can also be found in the objectives of subject area curricula. For description we find thinking skills such as: observe, identify recognize, label, name, locate, describe, compare, and contrast. For sequence we find: arrange events in sequence, note changes over time, predict, follow directions, use appropriate procedures, plan procedures. For choice we find: make decisions, select, identify issues, recognize problems, generate solutions, identify alternative solutions, solve problems. A wide variety of subject area curricula provide many examples of action situations which illustrate these thinking skills and these curricula are readily available to most teachers.

Many situational content objectives, then, aim to help the learner understand descriptions, sequences, and choices in a situation. And talk about description, sequence, and choice lends itself to language development, as we have seen. Therefore the implications for the language teacher who is teaching situational information are:

1. Look for patterns of description, sequence, and choice in the content objectives.
2. Where necessary, help communication by using appropriate graphics, objects, demonstrations, and so on.
3. Guide the students' development of the language of description, sequence, and choice as the students communicate about situational information.

3.8 THE STRUCTURE OF ACTION SITUATIONS

One main aim of this chapter was to show how a link could be made between language and the structure of action situations using flowcharts to represent description, sequence, and choice. Consequently the central idea of action needs to be given some more attention. As far as communicating about action is concerned, the flowchart is a simple picture of a series of actions (verbal and nonverbal), and description, sequence and choice are explications of aspects of the flowchart. Each diamond in the flowchart is a choice, each path through the flowchart is a sequence, and at any point on that path a description can be given of the immediate state of affairs. The flowchart is a way of talking about the broad outline of the action situation, and description, sequence, and choice begin to fill in some of the details. This is meant as a guideline to be used with common sense and intuitive flexibility. It is a communication technique to focus the central ideas of action situations without obscuring them with too much complexity or limiting them with too much rigor.

At the same time it is important to show how these simple distinctions fit into a general theory of action, to check that the distinctions are not ad hoc, to link them to a general and coherent framework, and to point out ways they can be extended in scope and detail. Von Wright in *Explanation and Understanding* (Von Wright, 1971) offers such a framework. He provides not only an explicit logical theory of action, but also locates it in a model of explanation for the social sciences which is clearly distinguished from causal explanation and explanation in the natural sciences and goes beyond the familiar concept of social rules. The central concepts are intentions and practical reasoning about goals, and these concepts are interlinked in the following way. Intentional human action can generally be seen as the product of practical reasoning, which is concerned with the necessary means to a given end of action. A intends to bring about q. A considers that p is a necessary means for q. Therefore A decides to do p. An explanation of goal-seeking strategies puts this in reverse. Why is A doing p? In order to bring about q. The concept of practical reasoning makes the distinction between someone who is following rules and merely behaving appropriately, and someone who is deliberating about choices and making decisions. Rule following does not require practical reasoning about choices; decision making does.

The central idea of an action situation is intentional action. To explore the decision situation which lies behind an intentional action is to reveal considerations of practical reasoning. The action situation is seen as a series of states of affairs affected by action (see Von Wright, 1971:43ff.). Description, sequence, and choice correspond to the state of affairs, the series of states of affairs, and the choice between alternative states of affairs. The action situation within the knowledge framework of our discussion is consistent with Von Wright's theory of practical reasoning. (For a further application of practical reasoning to language, see Mohan, 1974.)

3.9 SUMMARY
AND CONCLUSION

To date, the full potential of action situations for language and thinking development has been missed. Some writers have seen the learner in the action situation as merely a learner of stock verbal responses; to others, the learner is merely a learner of rules of language and appropriate conventions. When we view human choice as central to action situations (and even the most simple situation involves choice), we recognize that an action situation engages the learner in making reasoned choices about what to say and what to do. Developing the learner's ability to talk and learn about the reasons for acting goes well beyond the teaching of decontextualized dialogues. Rather, it demands contextualized dialogues and knowledge of the communicative environment of the learner. If we see the learner in an action situation as a decision maker who needs to both talk and act, then action situations can be used to provide the context for dialogue, encouraging the learner to communicate more effectively.

The action situation is analogous to a case study—it is the specific practical aspect of an activity. In our discussion we used an example of an action situation involving a particular shopper making a specific request. This is a specific, practical aspect of the activity of shopping. Situational dialogues and talk about the action situation are then practical discourse (i.e., discourse about the practical aspect of an activity), while knowledge of the action situation is called practical understanding (i.e., knowledge of the practical aspect of an activity).

Flowcharts are particularly useful for teachers wishing to develop practical understanding and practical discourse. In our discussion, we used them to show how action situations contain the three knowledge structures of description, sequence, and choice. In turn, each knowledge structure suggests possible classroom activities for its understanding, and relevant language items (grammatical, notional and functional) for language development.

The flowchart is a graphic aid to the second language learner for seeing the common structure of all action situations. It clearly shows that the language resources necessary to talk about description, sequence, and choice are common to all language situations, and that developing discourse about the three knowledge structures calls for a broad competence in the language.

To develop action situations more fully, the language teacher can draw on semantic grammars and adapt ideas from available teaching materials. But most importantly, since we wish to transfer language and thinking skills to other areas of learning, language teachers can find a profitable source of action situations for teaching in content curricula.

The three knowledge structures (description, sequence, and choice) of an action situation are a key to communication, discourse, and thinking across the curriculum. For both the language teacher and the content teacher, they provide a framework which makes possible the transfer of thinking skills and language skills to all areas of learning.

EXERCISES FOR
CHAPTER THREE

1. Consider some of the dialogues in any language teaching text you are familiar with. What do you consider to be some of the advantages and disadvantages of these dialogues? Are there any examples of talking heads dialogues? Are there any examples of dialogues embedded in an action context? How is the action context presented? What use is made of the action context during teaching and learning activities?

2. Find out a student's communicative network—the English language contacts the student makes in a typical day or week. With advanced students this can be done by asking them to write their name in the middle of a page and put the people they speak with around the edges of the page. More detailed information can be added by putting in the hours of contact, adding reading, writing, and mass media, etc.

3. Make a socio-topical matrix of the speech and social situations of interest to your students. The matrix will combine who will be spoken with and what will be spoken about. A class discussion is often a good way to get the required information.

4. Nelson and Winters, *ESL Operations*, present ways of working with operations or procedures for doing something, like operating a tape recorder. One student gives directions to another, who then does the operation. Make a list of some of the operations your students are familiar with and try one out in your classroom. Design a flowchart for the operation. Consider ways in which the language used could become more complex than a simple string of directions.

5. Urzua, *Talking Purposefully*, uses processes from the environment of the school, such as drawing a geometrical design in a math class as a base for talk and interaction activites with young children. List some content processes which capture your students' interest and consider ways to develop their language potential.

6. Action strips, comic strips, and cartoons are all popular ways to develop talk in the classroom. Blackboard stories are another way. Here, the teacher makes sketches on the board to give visual support to a story. Discuss how you would use any of these beyond a simple story line. Cartoons can be opportunities for cultural discussion and interpretation. Strips can be chosen to touch on real issues in students' lives. Teachers in history classes make imaginative use of period cartoons and posters to focus on complex social issues.

7. Consider ways you might help learners produce their own picture stories or photostories. Younger children may like to record their experiences on a field trip with a picture story that might be written up at a later stage. Barndt, Cristall, and Marino *Getting There*, show how adults can use the photostory or picture story to express important issues in their lives. The picture story may be a major form of popular literacy for some

students, as in Latin America, and you may wish to look into the role it plays in their literacy and their culture.

8. Analyze a total situation that your students are familiar with. Break it down into: (i) setting and people (description); (ii) routines and patterns (sequence); (iii) decisions and problems (choices, alternatives). Then consider some ways of working with parts of the situation in the classroom. Use a flowchart to sketch out the logical skeleton of the situation.

   The classroom itself is one example. J. Willis, *Teaching English through English*, discusses the classroom situation and suggests ways of using it for language teaching and learning. The classroom situation could be divided: (i) the classroom and the students; (ii) classroom procedures, lesson stages, ways of operating equipment; (iii) interruption (latecomers and things lost), control and discipline.

   A job is another example. *Industrial English*, pp.205–238, contains teaching materials for a job situation. Part 1 deals with the workplace setting and staff. Parts 2 and 3 cover processes, from the whole factory to the individual job. Parts 4 and 5 deal with safety and quality control problems.

9. Design a flowchart for any process, procedure, or situation from a content area. Suggest how you would use it in the language classroom. As a guide, use the section of this chapter that deals with flowcharts.

10. List some of the problems that your students face in their daily lives. Wallerstein, in *Language and Culture in Conflict*, a course for adult immigrants, mentions the general areas of the family, culture, and conflict, neighborhood, immigration, health, work, money. To identify problems she recommends careful listening and observing in the classroom, the community, students' homes, and discussions with community workers.

11. Look at the ways problems, decision situations, conflicts, or dilemmas are presented in pictures, strips, or flowcharts. Consider different kinds of material, advertisements and newspapers, as well as textbooks. Discuss how any of these ways might be used to present a problem or a choice for class discussion. Wallerstein, *Language and Culture in Conflict*, uses carefully chosen pictures as a basis for problem solving discussions; for instance, a picture of a mother asking her daughter to look after her young brother while the daughter says that she wants to play outside. Another approach is to stop a strip in the middle. The learners then discuss how to go on. One problem posing strip leads up to a father deciding whether or not to speak to a teacher who has punished his child. News photos are another alternative. One writing program uses a news photo of two New York detectives carrying a wounded fellow detective from a Muslim mosque in Harlem to a waiting automobile. They are protected by another detective with a gun from a taunting, screaming crowd.

   A different way of looking at problems comes from content area material. Long division in mathematics is often difficult for elementary students. The teacher presents a flowchart of how to solve long division calculations and acts it through with an actual calculation while the class suggest what is to be done. (This example was contributed by Sylvia Helmer.)

12. Look at the analysis of decision situations in any of the literature on decision making (e.g., More and Thomas, 1976, for decision making in business and industry). Choose a decision situation and describe how you would present it clearly to learners so that they can develop the language of decision making.

13. Find examples in discourse of description, sequence, and choice. List some of the language differences you find, considering grammar, language functions, and language notions.

14. Choose an action situation. Ask a speaker of English to describe the situation, narrate a process, and discuss a decision. Record what is said and identify some of the language differences you find.

15. Choose a situation and design a student exercise which calls for the language of description, sequence, or choice. Use as a guide the section of this chapter that deals with situations and discourse. Record the language that the learners use in the exercise and compare it with the listings of language items given in the section.

16. Find a subject area curriculum guide that states teaching objectives. (See the section of this chapter which deals with teaching situational information.) Find examples of objectives that relate to description, sequence, and choice. Now look at teaching materials which teach these objectives. Compare examples of the language of description, sequence, and choice.

CHAPTER THREE
SUGGESTED READINGS

Asher, J. 1977. *Learning Another Language Through Actions: The Complete Teacher's Guidebook.* Los Gatos: Sky Oaks Productions. Presents the learning strategy of Total Physical Response, where the learner learns a language by doing physical actions following teacher commands in the language. This relates language use to physical action in the immediate context.

Barndt, D., F. Cristall and D. Marino. 1982. *Getting There: Producing Photostories with Immigrant Women.* Toronto: Between the Lines. Presents photostories of immigrant women surviving in and adapting to a new culture. The women themselves produce their own stories by a process which starts from the issues of everyday life and encourages people to talk to each other about their experiences as a means of learning and taking action. Contains background essays and a step-by-step guide.

Corder, S.P. 1966. *The Visual Element in Language Teaching.* London: Longman. Emphasizes the role of the visual element as providing a context for language teaching and aiding student understanding.

Faerch, C. and G. Kasper (eds.). 1982. *Strategies in Interlanguage Communication.* London: Longman. Communication strategies are used when someone speaking a second language experiences a problem in communication and decides on a strategic plan for its solution. In this sense it is decision making in communication. The book defines communication strategies, describes empirical studies, and discusses problems in research.

Maley, A. and A. Duff. 1978. *Drama Techniques in Language Learning.* Cambridge: Cambridge University Press. Contains a wide selection of drama activities grouped under the headings of observation (e.g., observation of the room), interpretation (e.g., miming actions and guessing what they are), and iteraction (e.g., role plays).

Mollica, A. 1976. "Cartoons in the Language Classroom" *Canadian Modern Language Review* 32–34:424–44. Mollica classifies cartoon/comic strips and their possible uses in the language classroom.

Nelson, G. and T. Winters. 1980. *ESL Operations: Techniques for Learning While Doing.* Rowley,

Mass.: Newbury House. Deals with operations or procedures for doing something, using a natural sequence of events. Examples include: operating a tape recorder, using an index, touching your toes, making a cup of coffee, filling in a form. One student gives directions to another, who must complete the operation. Used particularly for practicing verb tenses.

Prabhu, N. 1983. *Procedural Syllabuses*. Singapore: SEAMEO Regional Language Centre, 18th Regional Seminar. Gives an account of the Communicational Teaching Project in South India, which follows a task-based syllabus. Each lesson is based on a task. Tasks include interpreting a schedule, interpreting a map or a set of rules; giving a set of directions; deciding which statement/ action is right and why; working out where it is cheaper to buy certain things, etc.

Urzua, C. 1981. *Talking Purposefully*. Silver Springs, Maryland: Institute of Modern Languages, Inc. An approach to second language work with young children based on a functional view of language use. Develops the language functions of self-expression, informing, persuading, and entertaining through activities from the environment of the school, such as a science experiment or the discussion of a geometrical design drawn in a math or art class.

Wallerstein, N. 1983. *Language and Culture in Conflict*. Reading, Mass.: Addison-Wesley. Based upon Brazilian educator Paulo Freire's problem-posing approach, the book suggests the development of an ESL curriculum from students' cultural conflicts, social needs, and fears in learning English and presents practical thematic classroom units covering such topics as immigration, health, family, and money.

Willis, J. 1982. *Teaching English through English*. London: Longman. The first part of this book covers the use of social, personal, and organizational language in typical classroom situations and helps teachers to see how these situations can be used for presenting, practicing, and reinforcing the target language. The aim is not only to teach English in English, but to exploit the genuine communicative situations that arise in the classroom for meaningful language practice (e.g., the physical conditions in the classroom, seating, books, and blackboard, tape recorders, and other equipment, interruptions).

Chapter 4

Language and Theoretical Knowledge

4.1 INTRODUCTION

Chapter 2 outlined a knowledge framework language teachers can use in organizing material. Chapter 3 discussed the specific, practical side of this framework, and in this chapter we will explore the general, theoretical or academic side. And because the knowledge framework was organized around an activity, this chapter will therefore develop the theoretical aspect of activities.

First and second language learners have difficulty with the presentation of theoretical, academic knowledge, since this knowledge is usually presented in verbal exposition, in textbooks and lectures. For the framework to be useful, therefore, it needs to help students gain access to theoretical knowledge.

We have seen that the theoretical aspect of an activity contains the three knowledge structures of classification, principles, and evaluation. Returning once again to the earlier insurance example, we saw that the newspaper articles classified types of insurance, explained causes of accidents, and evaluated drivers. In fact, classification, principles, and evaluation appear throughout theoretical, academic knowledge.

Because the importance of these knowledge structures in teaching lies in their potential for language development and for the transfer of learning across content areas, they must be related to language and thinking processes if they are to be useful in teaching.

The inquiry approach
to teaching

How can a teacher best help students deal with the demands of academic content classes such as the study of chemistry or history? A teacher needs to do more than help the students to work through a specific piece of content material. A more satisfactory aim is for the teacher to help students to manage content learning tasks independently. One way to do this is to give students not only detailed information but also a sense of the pattern or structure into which these details fit. That is, students gain both knowledge and an awareness of the structure of that knowledge. If students are more aware of the structure of knowledge, they are better equipped to manage content learning tasks independently.

In the field of curriculum development there is an approach known as the inquiry, discovery or thinking process approach. This approach bases curriculum design on the structure of the academic disciplines. As Jerome Bruner puts it in *The Process of Education*: "the curriculum of a subject should be determined by the most fundamental understanding that can be achieved of the underlying principles that give structure to that subject. Teaching specific topics or skills without making clear their context in the broader fundamental structure of a field of knowledge is uneconomical in several deep senses" (Bruner, 1960:31). Ignoring underlying principles is uneconomical since it makes it difficult for the student to generalize from what has been learned to what will be encountered later.

This inquiry or discovery approach was popular in various American curriculum projects in the 1960s. "Curriculum-builders of this period were primarily subject matter specialists who organized their materials around the primary structural elements of their respective disciplines: problems or concerns, key concepts, principles, and modes of inquiry" (McNeill, 1977:48). For example, *Science—A Process Approach* organizes science in the elementary school around such processes as observing, classifying, interpreting, and experimenting, using material drawn from various sciences to develop these processes. *Man: A Course of Study*, a famous example, leads students to examine the biological and social nature of man by observation, speculation, hypothesis-making, and hypothesis-testing. *The Taba Social Studies Curriculum* (Durkin, 1969) includes listing, grouping and labelling, as well as inferring, generalizing, and applying generalizations.

Turning our attention to language courses, a course in expository writing strongly influenced by the work of Jerome Bruner is *Writing as a Thinking Process* (Lawrence, 1972). It presents an inquiry or discovery method in which students ask questions of, manipulate, and extrapolate from data. For instance, to develop time sequence organization in writing, students are given a list of events which they manipulate into chronological order and then express in writing. In other words, a thinking process precedes the writing process. Lawrence's course is in keeping with the discovery approach in general, in which traditional course content becomes divided into its 'ingredients': data and the methods of inquiry. Students are expected to find out for themselves rather than being told. Lawrence's course includes definition, classification, cause-effect, hypothesis, generalization, proposals, and personal opinion.

There is an important distinction to be made between knowledge structures and thinking processes. Classification is a knowledge structure; classifying is a thinking process. Classifying is the process of working with a classification. If you classify books in a library, you are working with a library classification system. If you classify plants you are working with a botanical classification. Many of the thinking processes listed in inquiry courses are ways of working with classification, principles, and evaluation. To classify is to use a classification; to experiment is to test a principle; to judge is to apply evaluation criteria.

Any inquiry curriculum should therefore include both knowledge structures and thinking processes. Specifically, it should include classification, principles and evaluation, and their associated thinking processes, since these are common to all academic disciplines. The approach taken in this book is compatible with the inquiry approach. However, in actual practice, the inquiry curricula have concentrated on thinking processes and neglected knowledge structures. By contrast, this book emphasizes the importance of underlying knowledge structures.

Many curricula contain excellent material linked to important thinking processes. But often their general potential is not fully developed. Frequently it is not clear what the underlying knowledge structures are, or how they can be communicated to learners. Nor is it shown how these knowledge structures are connected with either thinking processes or with language.

The example in the next section fills these gaps. We show how classification, principles, and evaluation apply to the case of nutrition. Classification, principles, and evaluation are communicated through tables and line graphs, keyed to associated thinking processes, and related to language. The example shows the connections between these different elements, and the connections are illustrated for each knowledge structure. In the case of classification, we describe the data students work with and the inquiry activities they apply to this data. Then we discuss the general form of the graphics used to represent classification, showing how this general form applies to any classification. Finally we illustrate the language for talking and writing about any classification. Principles and evaluation are treated similarly.

The example aims not only to teach the learner about a body of information but also to develop independence in learning by helping the learner to work with classification, principles, and evaluation in general. Adapted appropriately, the ideas in the following example can be applied very widely to other subject areas and topics.

4.2 A UNIT OF ACADEMIC CONTENT: NUTRITION*

Assume we are teaching a class in nutrition where we want a transfer of thinking and language development.

Classification

Data and tasks

The first student tasks are observing and measuring. The students are asked to put their bag lunches on their desks and they describe each of them, with help from the

---

* The nutrition unit was developed with the help of the considerable combined classroom experience of Bridget Bruneski, Nick Collins, Margaret Early, Eileen LeGallais, Ann Shorthouse, and Eileen Yeung in Vancouver, Canada.

teacher where necessary. The teacher draws a table like Figure 4.1 on the blackboard and writes in the information as it develops. The pupils are listed down the side of the table and the kinds of food across the top.

The next activities are grouping and labelling. The lunch food is categorized according to Canada's Food Guide. The teacher and class now take the various kinds of food that have been mentioned, list them down the side of Figure 4.2, and discuss how they fit with the food categories listed across the top of the table. Finally the students are told the daily amounts of the various types of food recommended for adolescents, which is given in the table of Canada's Food Guide Amounts. In itself, this is simply information-giving, but it plays a role later on.

Figure 4.1

Classification: *Observing and Measuring*
Students put their lunches on the desk and the class
describes them.

		Apples	Oranges	Bread ...
Name:	Peter	1		2 slices
	Mary		1	3 slices
	Sarbjit	1		1 slice

Figure 4.2

Classification: *Grouping and Labelling*
Categorize the lunch food according to Canada's Food Guide categories.

	Milk	Vegetables	Meat & Fish	Fruit	Bread & Cereals	Other
Apple				X		
Carrot		X				
Tuna			X			

Figure 4.3

Classification: *Canada's Food Guide Amounts*

Milk	Vegetables	Meat & Fish	Fruit	Bread & Cereals
32 oz. 4 glasses	1 cup	6 oz.	2 (apples)	4 slices

KEY GRAPHICS FOR CLASSIFICATION

Classification deals with objects/individuals/items which form classes/concepts/ definitions on the basis of their characteristics/attributes/properties.

Figure 4.4
Classification Table

| | Characteristics | | | | |
	a	b	c	d	etc.
Items #1	X		X		
#2		X	X		
#3	X		X		
etc.					

Figure 4.5
Classification Tree or Graph

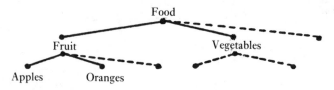

General form of graphics

The activities above show how lunch food can be described and classified. What about classifying other things, such as the contents of students' desks, bags, or pockets, or in fact any set of objects of interest? This is simply a matter of erasing the words and information from the table and writing in new labels and information. In other words, tables used for classification have a general form which is adapted to particular instances. To classify is to form groups of objects/individuals/items into classes/concepts/ definitions on the basis of characteristics/attributes/properties. Figure 4.4 shows this general form by having objects along one side and the characteristics along the other. It is the general form of Figures 4.1 and 4.2 and can be used for organizing the data to be classified or for presenting the results of a classification. Classification can also be expressed by a tree (or line graph), with objects at the bottom and characteristics or classes on the higher nodes, as shown here in Figures 4.5.

Relation to language

As the students classify information and express it in tables, there will be talk. What kind of talk might be involved in producing the table and expressing what is in the table? What further sorts of language does this provide occasions to develop?

With the first entry in Figure 4.1. we might have: *This is an apple, Peter has an apple.* These are various rather pedestrian ways of expressing meanings connected with the first entry or cell—the relation between *Peter, I,* and *apples.*

The table contains a set of meanings which can be packed, unpacked, and built upon; and language provides various ways to express those meanings. "Is" is used here in its sense of class membership, exactly what one might expect in the activity of classification; "an" indicates singular or one, which fits in with the activity of measurement. The "have" of possession links together what is being described, connecting the individual with the characteristics. Class membership, quantity, and possession are all language notions. Notions are meanings that can be expressed in various ways in English. They are listed in reference grammars organized by meaning. So if we want to show how language relates to these activities, we need to show the relation between the thinking processes, typical sentences, and the meanings or notions expressed, keyed to a reference grammar.

This is the intention behind Figure 4.6, where the thinking process of measuring shows up in the "three" of the example sentences. "Three" is also linked to the notion of amount or quantity, which is treated in the *Communicative Grammar of English* (Leech and Svartvik, 1975:48ff.), to give just one example. (References to Leech and Svartvik—

Figure 4.6

Classification: *Thinking Processes and Language*

Thinking process	Notional language
Observing/Measuring/ Describing	*This is an apple. Mary has three slices of bread.* POINTER WORDS (GCE:58): this/that VERBS OF CLASS MEMBERSHIP: be VERBS OF POSSESSION: have POSSESSIVES: his GENITIVES: Mary's REFERRING TO OBJECTS (GCE:43ff) Singular/plural, count/mass, part/whole, articles AMOUNT OR QUANTITY (GCE:48): some/two/half UNIT NOUNS (GCE:45): piece/lump NOUNS OF MEASURE (GCE:45): a pound of/a pint of
Comparison	*Mary has more bread than Sarbjit.* COMPARISON (GCE:104): more than/taller (cf. WATP Comparison and Contrast)
Classification	*Apples are a kind of fruit.* GENERIC FORMS (GCE:53): apples/music SPECIES NOUNS (GCE:45): kind/sort/species/class CLASSIFICATION: be/include/place under (cf. WATP Classification)

CGE—are given in Figure 4.6 when a notion may not be self-explanatory). In addition, there are references to *Writing as a Thinking Process* (Lawrence, 1972—WATP—, which explicitly treats thinking processes as units of a language course. The thinking processes mentioned form a group associated with classification. They can all be seen as aspects of constructing, expressing, or commenting on a classification table, as the example sentences in Figure 4.6 bear out. This is another illustration of the key role of the graphic, a point which will be discussed further. Comparison is not a thinking process mentioned in the previous student activities, nor is it something which is specifically expressed by the table. It is an example of further development of language using the table as a point of departure.

Principles (cause-effect)

Data and tasks

In the classification section, what was classified was the students' own food. The natural follow through for the cause-effect section would be to do nutritional experiments.

First, teacher and students set up an experiment where two mice eat different diets for three weeks. (This example is for illustration only. I do not in any way wish to recommend experiments on animals.) One mouse has a balanced diet, the other has a sugar and soft drink diet. At the end of three weeks the students observe the differences in appearance and energy between the two mice. The result can then be written up as in Figure 4.7. A more limited, but easier experiment would be to place an old tooth (or the equivalent) in a beaker containing a certain soft drink and to put another, for comparison, in a beaker of water. The first tooth should begin to dissolve, conveying an unmistakable message to regular fans of the soft drink. The results can be written up in a pattern similar to Figure 4.7.

Human nutritional effects are presented directly to the students. The effects of an imbalanced diet on the human body is explained through a cause-effect format as in Figure 4.9. Nutrition texts will often provide pictures to fill out this type of description.

It will have been noticed that in these tables "cause" has been treated as "conditions", following the view that causal relations are matters of necessary and/or sufficient conditions. In the present simple and crude description, conditions have been described en bloc, and so have effects. A finer description would separate out each condition and each effect so that the pattern of relationships between conditions and effects can be analyzed, and students can get a clearer view of the main point of the experiments. Figure 4.8 does this for Figure 4.7.

Since the purpose of these activities is to create an awareness of the general relation between diet and the human body, it is important for the class to develop a generalization about this relationship that goes beyond the individual descriptions of dietary deficiencies. With the mouse experiment table, a low-level generalization such as: *if a mouse eats sugar, then it becomes unhealthy* can be written across the top of the table; the "if" clause can be put on the conditions side and the remainder on the effects side.

PRINCIPLES (CAUSE AND EFFECT)

Figure 4.7

Cause and Effect: *An experiment where two mice eat different diets*

	Conditions	Effects
Mouse 1	Balanced diet	good appearance, high energy
Mouse 2	sugar/soft drink diet	poor appearance, low energy

Figure 4.8
Cause and Effect: *Diet*

	Balanced	Sugar	High Energy
Mouse 1	X		X
Mouse 2		X	

KEY GRAPHICS FOR PRINCIPLES

Cause-effect deals with conditional relations between states of affairs occurring in time sequence.

Figure 4.9

Cause and Effect: *The effects of an imbalanced diet on humans*

	Conditions	Effects
Diet 1	not enough protein	poor growth
Diet 2	not enough milk and cheese	poor bones and teeth

Figure 4.10

Cause-Effect Table

	Generalization	
	Conditions	Effects
Case 1	state of affairs at time 1	state of affairs at time 2
Case 2		

Figure 4.11
Condition-Effect Table

	Possible Conditions			Effect(s)
	A	B	C	D
Case 1	X			X
Case 2		X		

Figure 4.12

Condition-Effect Tree

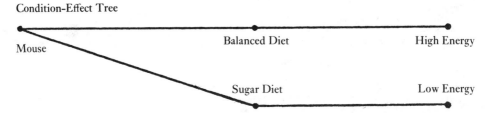

General form of graphics

Just as the classification table can be used in its general form for a variety of classifications, so the cause-effect table can be used for many different cause-effect relations. Cases are written down the side of the table and conditions and effects across the top, with the generalization written above them.

We should analyze cause and effect by considering a series of cases and look for connections between conditions and effects. For each case we should describe the state of affairs at a particular time and the state of affairs at a later time, attempting to identify all of the relevant conditions for the effect. (See Figures 4.10, 4.11 and 4.12.)

Relation to language

As the students put together a table like Figure 4.7 they might say *I think the mouse is tired because he has been eating sugar*, inferring a condition from an effect. Alternatively, they might say *This mouse has a balanced diet and so probably will stay healthy*, reversing the inference and predicting an effect from a condition. If they are going beyond the particular cases observed, they might say *If a mouse eats sugar then it becomes unhealthy* or (very formally) *If the healthy mouse were to eat sugar, then it would become unhealthy*, formulating hypotheses about observed conditions and effects. Or they might say *If animals do not have a balanced diet, their health is affected in many ways*, generalizing about a given cause-effect relationship.

The general cause-effect table contains cases, conditions, effects, and generalizations, and the students' remarks can be seen as making various relations between these elements. The thinking processes listed in Figure 4.13 form a group of operations connected with developing a cause-effect table just as the classification group of thinking processes were related to the classification table.

As before, the meanings or notions shown in the example sentences are identified and keyed to a reference grammar in Figure 4.13. It is hardly accidental that these meanings are the ones to be expressed: cause, condition, generalization are components of cause-effect tables.

The pattern for cause-effect can be generalized to other kinds of principles (means-end, methods and techniques, rules, norms and strategies). To analyze a cause-effect relation is to work out what conditions are necessary and sufficient to result in an effect. Similarly, to analyze a principle is to work out the necessary and/or sufficient conditions for a principle to operate. For instance, a country could have a citizenship law which states that you may become a citizen if you have lived in that country for at least three

Figure 4.13
Cause and Effect: *Thinking Processes and Language*

Thinking process	Notional language
Inferring conditions from effects	*I think* the mouse is tired *because* he has been eating sugar. ATTITUDES TO TRUTH (CGE: 132). I know/doubt/believe/assume CAUSE/REASON (CGE: 93) is due to/the result of/because of (cf. WATP Making Inferences)
Predicting effects of conditions	*This mouse has a balanced diet and so probably will stay healthy.* PREDICTION (CGE: 131) must/ought to/should/I bet/ therefore/consequently PROBABILITY (CGE: 131) probably/maybe/it is probable/ likely (cf. WATP Prediction)
Formulating hypotheses about conditions and effects	*If a mouse eats sugar, then it gets unhealthy. If the healthy mouse were to eat sugar, then it would get unhealthy.* CONDITION AND CONTRAST (CGE: 96) if/unless/ otherwise/in that case/then . . . although/in spite of HYPOTHETICAL MEANING (CGE: 124) were/would (cf. WATP Hypothesis)
Generalizing about a given cause-effect relationship	*If they do not have a balanced diet, the health of all animals is affected in many ways.* *For example, the mouse that drank Zapp lacks energy.* WORDS OF GENERAL OR INCLUSIVE MEANING (CGE: 50) and SCALE OF AMOUNT (CGE: 51) all, every, everyone, always, none, nobody, never, completely SUMMARY AND GENERALIZATION, EXPLANATION (CGE: 157) in short/to sum up, for example, for instance. (cf. WATP Generalization and Specifics)

years and have no criminal record. *Three years residence* and *no criminal record* are necessary conditions for the right to become a citizen. What this amounts to is using the cause-effect table with a change of headings to analyze principles of other kinds.

Evaluation

Data and tasks

For an evaluation task, each student keeps a personal record of his/her day's intake of food according to the Food Guide categories. The student then evaluates the intake by comparing the amounts with the Canada Food Guide recommended amounts. The evaluation is therefore a matter of judging an item by comparison with the recommended standards. The graphic representation for this is shown in Figure 4.14.

Figure 4.14

EVALUATION : *Of items*
Student keeps a personal record of daily food intake and evaluates it by comparing it with Canada's Food Guide.

	Fruit	Vegetables	Evaluation
Day 1	low	adequate	good amounts of vegetables but lacking in fruit
Day 2	none	adequate	

Criteria (header over Fruit, Vegetables)

Figure 4.15

Evaluation: *Of choices*

Student considers possible choices for tomorrow's lunch and decides to take action on one.

	Action	Outcomes	Evaluation
Choice 1	go to McTavish's (hamburger, chips, soft drink)	weight gain possible tooth decay higher cost, less effort	an easy choice, but bad for health and pocket.
Choice 2	bring own lunch (peanut butter sandwich, apple, milk)	weight loss lower cost more effort	more difficult, but cheaper and better for health.

KEY GRAPHICS FOR EVALUATION

Evaluation deals with evaluations of objects/cases on the basis of criteria/reasons by reference to standards/outcomes in regard to potential benefits. Grading in value can be shown by listing items in rank order.

Figure 4.16

	Criteria			Evaluation
	a	b	. . .	on criteria a, b . . .
Item 1	−	+		good/bad/neutral
Item 2	−	+		

Figure 4.17

	Actions			Outcomes			Evaluation
	A	B	. . .	C	D	. . .	for reasons X, Y, Z
Case 1	X			X			good/bad/neutral
Case 2		X			X		

Figure 4.18

Decision Tree

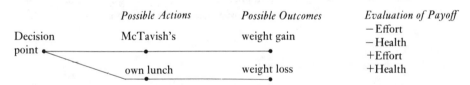

	Possible Actions	*Possible Outcomes*	*Evaluation of Payoff*
Decision point	McTavish's	weight gain	− Effort − Health
	own lunch	weight loss	+Effort +Health

Students can also judge choices. Each student considers the possible choices for the next day's lunch, with the likely outcomes of each choice. The student then evaluates the outcomes against goals and values in order to make a decision. Figure 4.15 compares the outcomes of eating the typical lunch at the local fast food place with bringing a self-prepared lunch of better food. Evaluation in this case requires the decision maker to weigh health and general well being, cost, and effort, to name the most obvious values and goals. The lunch decision should be a reflection of general nutrition policy, and the final task should be a discussion of the general implications of this decision for one's usual eating habits.

General form of graphics

There are two forms of tables here. Figure 4.16 is for making judgments on objects/ items/individuals, and Figure 4.17 is for making judgments on cases/actions and outcomes. The left section of each table describes items or cases; the right section evaluates them. If the evaluation section of each table is ignored for the moment, it will be seen that Figure 4.16 is similar to a classification table, and Figure 4.17 is very similar to a cause-effect table.

The evaluation sections of Figures 4.16 and 4.17 are a matter of judging the merit of items or actions-and-outcomes. At its simplest, each item or each case is judged good, neutral, or bad. (For simplicity, degrees of goodness or badness have been ignored.) In the case of the students' daily diet, this judgment is made by comparison with a standard (Canada's Food Guide); in the case of the lunch decision it is made by considering costs and benefits. In both cases we are looking for health benefits, and this agrees with a general view that evaluations are made with a view to certain outcomes in regard to potential costs and benefits. The daily diet evaluation is standardized, so that it is easy to state the evaluation criteria explicitly beforehand. The lunch decision is more open-ended however.

It is usual to distinguish between evaluation (assessing the merits of an item or action) and grading (putting items or actions in order of comparative merit). This is the familiar distinction between making an evaluative comment on a student's work and giving it a mark or grade. The grading of objects and actions (ranking them or placing them in order of preference) can be shown by putting them into rank order down the side of a table. (Here, *degrees* of goodness come into play.) This is often done in charts rating products in consumer magazines. Finally, evaluation in these activities covers not only the assessment of merit, consideration of criteria or reasons, and grading, but also choice or decision. While some choices can be routine and impersonal, decisions about what we eat also involve personal values and cultural norms.

Figure 4.19
Evaluation: *Thinking Processes and Language*

Thinking Process	Notional Language
Evaluating objects on some criteria by reference to standards and ranking of objects	*That day's diet is <u>unsatisfactory</u> because there is not <u>enough</u> milk. I <u>prefer</u> Tuesday's diet.* DESCRIBING EMOTIONS (CGE: 137) satisfactory/ unsatisfactory, approve/ disapprove, like/dislike INVOKING STANDARDS good/bad, etc. ROLE, STANDARD, VIEWPOINT (CGE: 103) enough/too PREFERENCE (CGE: 139) prefer/had rather, had, sooner
Evaluating possible actions on some grounds and on one course of action	*I <u>ought</u> to bring my own lunch because I <u>want</u> to lose weight.* VOLITION (CGE: 141) want/wish/intend/aim. PERMISSION and OBLIGATION (CGE: 143) Can, may, must, have to, need, should, had better INVOKING STANDARDS right/wrong, etc. (cf. WATP Proposals, Discussion)

Relation to language

The thinking processes in Figure 4.19 are all associated with rational choice. Making a rational choice about tomorrow's lunch, a student might say "I want to make my own lunch rather than buy one at McTavish's because I ought to lose weight." Nonarbitrary choice ("I want") implies preference ranking of alternatives (x rather than y). Preference ranking implies an assessment or judgment based on the relevant characteristics of the choices or on the consequences of the choice ("because"). Rational choice also involves relevant notions. Choice (VOLITION) implies preference (PREFERENCE) ranking of alternatives (COMPARISON), which in turn implies an assessment of merit (STANDARDS) on reasoned grounds (REASON). Since rational choice springs from a person's evaluative attitudes and feelings towards the alternatives, it relates to the section of notional grammar that deals with the emotions and attitudes of the speaker.

4.3 GRAPHICS AND COMMUNICATION OF CLASSIFICATION, PRINCIPLES, EVALUATION

The nutrition example used simple graphics to communicate about classification, principles, and evaluation. There are two aims in using graphics for this purpose. The first aim is to communicate particular information; in this example, to communicate about a classification of food. The second aim is more important and more general: it is to communicate the structure of knowledge, for example, to communicate about classification in general. The second aim provides for transfer of learning in order to help students communicate about classification in all subject areas.

The tables created by students can be used for communication in many ways. The following suggestions go from controlled to less controlled tasks.

(i) Converting completed tables into speech or writing.
A student reads a row across a table and converts it into a spoken or written sentence: *Peter has an apple and two slices of bread. If you do not have enough protein, you will have poor growth.* The same can be done for columns down a table: *Peter has an apple and Sarbjit has an apple.* Pairs of columns or rows can be used for comparison and contrast practice: *The first mouse has a balanced diet but the second mouse has a sugar and soft drink diet.* The sentence pattern used for each row can be the same, or the student can be encouraged to vary it. Paragraphs or larger units speech or writing can be developed from whole tables.

(ii) Filling in partly completed or empty tables.
The student fills in an empty cell or a row across a table. Like filling in forms, this gives the student the support of a framework while making minimal language demands. (In fact a form is very like an empty row in a table, and a

number of completed forms assembled together make up a table). Partly completed tables can be used for slot and filler work with beginning students.

(iii)   Using tables to prompt questions.

Students can make up questions about a completed table (*How many people brought apples for lunch?*), or they can fill in tables by interviewing other students about the necessary information.

(iv)   Using tables to provide the basic information for role play and drama.

For instance, using the table about diet and diet deficiencies, students can act out a scene between a patient with a nutrition problem and a doctor. Or again, using the table about the decision on lunch choices, students can role play an argument about the kind of lunch to have.

In all of the above cases, further support can of course be given by providing additional language; e.g., with comparison and contrast, terms like *similar*, *different*, *but*, *also*, *both* and model sentences can be provided with the table.

It might seem redundant to suggest that students should be encouraged to take advantage of tables and line graphs present in the texts they have to deal with, but a frequent finding in reading research is that students attend to the written text and ignore the tables and line graphs that go with it. Yet tables and line graphs are often strategically chosen by authors and can be very important, if not central, in conveying information in content textbooks. Perhaps the high point of this tendency is in geography where sketch-map geography and the atlas convey very little content by words alone. It may be valuable to help students become more aware of tables and diagrams by collecting and discussing examples from textbooks and from everyday reading.

One standard task that students face is demonstrating their comprehension of a chapter or lecture by writing answers to questions. An alternative to such questions, and a convenient way to reach the same goal, is for students to fill out a table or line graph. If the chapter or lecture contrasts two different geographic regions, for instance, it is common to get students to fill in information in a table contrasting the regions by relief, vegetation, climate, and so on. This has several advantages. It initially lowers the level of language skill required so that students can demonstrate what they know more readily. It also focuses attention on the larger structure of the information. It saves teacher time in writing out questions. And, it avoids the trap of asking trivial and unconnected questions simply as a test of comprehension.

Showing what you know by making up or filling out a table or line graph is also an alternative to the various writing tasks that face students. To continue the geography example, instead of writing an essay comparing and contrasting two regions, the student can express the same information in a table. Of course, this is not to say that the student is never to do extended writing. Making up or filling out tables can be an intermediate stage. At a later stage tables can be converted into speech or writing, as has already been discussed.

A very simple use of the line graph for composition has been called the 'pattern note'. The title of a topic is written in the center of a sheet of paper and ideas are developed on dividing branches radiating out from it, providing a rudimentary map of thoughts about the topic. The pattern note can be developed by an individual or a group and can be a summary of thought and discussion or can be a rough plan for talk or writing. The example in Figure 4.20 is a slightly modified part of a pattern note produced by a group of long term prisoners about problems they faced in prison (see Priestley et al, 1978:29).

Finally, tables and line graphs can be used by teachers as a way of previewing (or reviewing) content. The simplest way to do this is to give a structured overview: the teacher decides on the key terms or concepts in the reading material or other content, puts them on the blackboard, and discusses the relations between them, drawing a line to show a connection between two concepts. The structured overview has been developed and tested on native speakers with good results by Earle (1978), who produced the example given in Figure 4.20.

Comparison of the pattern note with the structured overview shows how they are variations on the same theme of indicating relations between concepts by drawing connecting lines. They are both line graphs. The main difference is the orderliness and precision of the structured overview compared to the unruly proliferation of the pattern note, which is only what one might expect from their different uses.

Summarizing, tables and line graphs can be used not only as an aid to understanding or producing text, but also as a general orientation to, or summary of content. We are not suggesting that tables and line graphs be used merely to stimulate talk; content teachers use them as ways to communicate about academic knowledge. Therefore, it is important to have a general understanding of how academic knowledge is represented through graphics.

Classification, principles, and evaluation are structures of relations fundamental to knowledge. Classifications are relations of class-inclusion, principles are conditional relations, and evaluation consists of relations of rating or ranking. These relations

Figure 4.20

Relations between Concepts

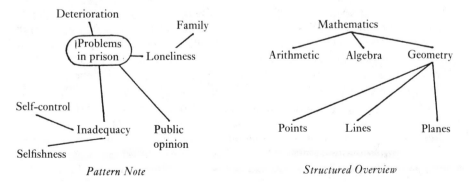

Pattern Note   Structured Overview

were represented here very simply by tables and line graphs. This simple approach can be elaborated and extended to many other aspects of the structure of academic knowledge. Detailed analysis of graphic representations of the structure of knowledge can be found in the literature of general research methodology.

Kerlinger (1973:60–70), reviewing the foundations of scientific research, states that science is not a knowledge of mere particulars, but rather of the way in which classes are related. Scientific knowledge is knowledge of relations between classes (or sets or variables), of the relation between smoking and cancer, for instance. Research determines the relations which hold between classes, sets, or variables. These relations can be represented equivalently by equations, graphs on a coordinate diagram, tables, or line graphs. Research studies usually present their results in one or another of these forms. Thus scientific knowledge is knowledge of relations, and these relations are represented precisely by equations, coordinate graphs, tables, and line graphs.

Much of academic knowledge is knowledge of relations, and these relations can be, and often are, represented by graphics. If learners are able to interpret these graphics, they have easier access to the knowledge represented. If teachers consider the relations they wish to communicate, they may well be able to communicate them by extending their current use of graphics.

4.4 THINKING PROCESSES
AND CLASSIFICATION,
PRINCIPLES, EVALUATION

Classification, principles, and evaluation apply across subject areas. This can be seen by examining the thinking processes listed in various subject area curricula. Therefore, it is important for teachers to convey the structures of classification, principles, and evaluation if they wish to help students transfer knowledge to new material.

In the nutrition example, classification, principles and values were related to thinking processes that appeared in inquiry curricula. For example, one knowledge structure, classification, was used in the first section of the nutrition unit. As we have noted, among other cognitive processes, *Science—A Process Approach* contains classifying, observing, and measuring. Another inquiry or process skills curriculum, the *Taba Social Studies Curriculum* contains listing, grouping, and labelling. In the discussion of the nutrition unit, it was suggested that these thinking processes could be seen as aspects of constructing or commenting on a classification table. In effect, the concept of classification is central and the various thinking processes mentioned are aspects of this fundamental idea. The basic elements of classifications are items, characteristics, and classes, and the table relates these in a clear way. The table is used as a way of displaying and sorting the data; it also is used as a way of showing the results of the analysis.

In the nutrition unit, students are not only learning to classify food, they are also learning the structure of classification. Learners can then transfer this structure and its associated thinking processes to new material. An essential point about the classifica-

Figure 4.21

Thinking Processes in Subject Curricula

Structures of knowledge	Thinking processes
Classification	Classifying, defining, using operational definitions. Understanding, applying or developing concepts, definitions or classifications.
Principles	Explaining and predicting. Interpreting data and drawing conclusions. Formulating, testing, and establishing hypotheses. Understanding, applying, or developing generalizations (causes, effects, means, ends, motives, reasons, rules, norms, strategies, methods, techniques, impacts, influences, responses, results).
Evaluation	Evaluating, ranking, appreciating, judging and criticizing. Forming, expressing and justifying preferences and personal opinions. Understanding, analyzing and deciding on goals, values, policies, and evaluation criteria.

tion table is that it conveys the structure of classification to learners. And they can adapt the table for different material. If students are not aware of the structure of classification they are less likely to be able to transfer understandings to new material. The same can be said for the structure of principles and the structure of evaluation.

We have noted that classification, principles, and values relate to many of the thinking processes listed in different subject area curricula. Figure 4.21 provides a guide to identifying these thinking processes.

Subject matter curricula which list thinking processes also contain a large number of suggestions for inquiry tasks which can be used in the language classroom. These tasks offer ways of working with knowledge structures and thinking processes for different levels of students and different areas of interest. For instance, there are many ways of working with principles and hypothesis-testing. These range from experiments in the natural and social sciences to very simple devices such as putting a mystery object in a box which can be handled and shaken.

For teachers interested in pursuing this approach, detailed analysis of the structure of classification, principles, and evaluation is found in work on logic, philosophy, and the research methodology of various disciplines. The concept of classification has received a considerable amount of attention from philosophers, logicians, and scientists. For a convenient review of work on classification as it relates to the particular case of geography, for example, see Harvey (1969:326ff). For present purposes, Harvey's review provides an analysis of the fundamentals of classification and shows the connections between the various forms of classification, clarifying the transition from simple to complex. We are here interested in the logical structure of simple classifications rather than the purposes of classification and the pitfalls in procedures for classifying.

The cause-effect type of principle has also received a great deal of attention in the logic and philosophy of science literature. In the nutrition unit we were concerned with cause and effect as it relates to experiments, and this issue is often approached through the discussion of various methods of experimental enquiry, usually known as Mill's methods, after John Stuart Mill. Following Von Wright (1960), we dealt with conditions (strictly speaking necessary and/or sufficient conditions), rather than causes, and see the methods as ways of finding the necessary or sufficient conditions for a given effect.

The format of the tables used to discuss principles (Figures 4.10 and 4.11) is a very simple form of the analysis of Skyrms (1966). Skyrms' presentation is a clear account of the fundamentals of Mill's methods. For a perspective on how this view of causal relations connects with causal explanation, teleological explanation, and explanation in history and the social sciences, see Von Wright (1971).

Evaluation is a topic of concern to ethics and the philosophy of value rather than the philosophy of science, although it is prominent in a number of social sciences, particularly economics. There is much less consensus in the analysis of values than in the two previous concepts, and I have attempted to follow Rescher (1969) closely. Rescher gives a comprehensive account of value theory. Again, this chapter presents only a simple logical structure in table form for evaluation. A more rigorous development of the topic can be found in the references given.

The thinking process curricula mentioned earlier are valuable for their wealth of detailed practical suggestions, but they seldom provide an analysis of the thinking processes or the knowledge structures they incorporate. We have seen that fundamentals can often be clearly presented to learners through tables and diagrams. In fact, such tables and diagrams are familiar and widely used, occurring naturally, so to speak, in everyday reading material, and are used deliberately in language teaching materials.

My point, however, is not to recommend that tables be used, since they already are, but to recommend that tables be designed systematically to develop greater understanding of fundamental knowledge structures.

Again, basic knowledge structures like classification, principles, and evaluation are hardly unfamiliar, particularly to teachers of content material, but often they are so familiar that they are submerged. Tables and diagrams counter-balance these tendencies by bringing the knowledge structure to the fore. The importance of knowledge structures is that they provide an understanding of fundamentals and aid in transfer. Because knowledge structures aid in the transfer of understanding, they should also be an important focus of the language teacher.

4.5 LANGUAGE DEVELOPMENT AND CLASSIFICATION, PRINCIPLES, EVALUATION

It is often the case that second language learners appear to be fluent in English but are unable to manage academic discourse. They are not able to read their textbooks easily, and their written essays are poor. They need to develop competence in academic discourse in order to get access to knowledge and to express what they know. Their difficulties with academic discourse are not surprising, however, since many native speakers of English show similar problems.

The strategy described in this chapter, and in other parts of this book, is for the teacher to express subject matter in graphics and then use the graphics to develop the language needed to express the subject matter. So a teacher might select subject material with a generalizable structure, such as classification, and create a graphic, such as a classification tree. The teacher might then work with students, using the graphic to help them write a paragraph about the subject material. Finally, the teacher would help students generalize and transfer their language learning by using classification trees with different subject material.

The general strategy mentioned above is a two-step process. In the first step, the teacher analyzes subject material for classification, principles, and evaluation and then designs graphics to express this material. In the second step, the teacher uses the graphic to develop competence in academic discourse. This chapter has emphasized the first step. The aim has been to show how teachers can analyze academic subject material they are familiar with, communicate it, develop general thinking processes, and develop language learning in the context of learning subject matter.

There are a large number of texts for students in the field of English for specific purposes. These aim to help second-language learners develop competence in academic discourse in particular subject areas. They are especially valuable for the second step, since they provide many examples of the use of graphics for developing connected discourse. Teachers can use these examples as models for their own techniques and materials. It would be helpful for a teacher to review, for instance, *Scope Stage 2* (Levine, 1970), *Nucleus General Science* (M. Bates and T. Dudley-Evans, 1976), and *English in Physical Science* (J. Allen and H. Widdowson, 1974).

While these materials provide many particular examples, it is important to see how graphics can develop a general competence in academic discourse. The graphics which aid the development of academic discourse are those that represent the structure of academic knowledge. Competence in academic discourse calls for the language to talk, read, and write about classification, principles, and evaluation in all subject areas; it calls for language to express the structure of knowledge.

The language to express the structure of knowledge can be divided roughly into three levels of probable difficulty:

1. *Language to express the meaning of a graphic of a knowledge structure.* This is required when learners say what a graphic means. In the nutrition unit, the classification table (Table 4.4) and classification tree (Figure 4.5) conveyed the basic relations of classification: class membership and class attributes. *Is* and *have* are simple ways of expressing these relations in English. The graphic for principles conveyed conditional relations. These can simply be expressed by *if, then, so,* and *because.* The graphic for evaluation conveyed relations of ranking or rating according to values. These can be simply expressed by *good, bad, better, right, wrong.* Initially learners can talk about these fundamental relations in simple language; later they can use more elaborate terms such as *attribute, factor,* and *attitude.*

2. *Language for the discussion or creation of a graphic.* This is required when learners discuss a graphic and engage in relevant thinking processes. Examples are given in

Figures 4.6, 4.13, and 4.19. This includes ways of giving and eliciting information, such as statements and questions; and judgments of truth and falsehood, such as ways of expressing possibility and certainty. It also includes pragmatic attitudes of the speaker and hearer, such as suggesting and advising.

3. *Language for converting a graphic into connected discourse.* This is required when learners convert a graphic into a written paragraph. Here the learner needs to know how to link sentences together (e.g., by using linkers such as *moreover, consequently, nevertheless*) and how to present and focus information (e.g., by using subordinate clauses).

We can offer a general explanation of the link between a graphic which conveys meanings and a connected discourse which expresses these meanings. A meaning or semantic relation such as class inclusion can be conveyed visually by a graphic, or it can be expressed verbally in discourse. In this chapter we have used two equivalent kinds of graphs: tables and line graphs. Tables or line graphs convey semantic relations because they are formal representations of semantic relations. This is explicitly stated in mathematical work in graph theory (see for instance, Ore, 1963:81). The verbal expression of such meanings or semantic relations is described in notional or semantic grammars.

A notional or semantic grammar of English classifies items of the English language according to the meanings they express. Leech and Svartvik (1975:12) make a useful distinction between four types of meaning or meaning organization. The first type is notional or conceptual meaning which includes categories like amount and time to describe aspects of our experience of the world. The second is information, reality and belief: that is, logical communication where categories like statements, questions and responses, possibility and certainty, affirmation and denial are used to make judgments about truth and falsehood and to give and elicit information about the world. The third is mood, emotion and attitude: the attitudes and behavior of the speaker and hearer, the interactional aspect of communication. This includes both the expression of feeling (e.g., by emotive emphasis in speech) and influencing the hearer by suggestions or threats. Fourthly, there is the organizational aspect of communication: the ordering and relating of our thoughts into connected discourse with appropriate focus and emphasis.

There is an approximate correspondence between Leech and Svartvik's types of meaning and the three levels of language to express the structure of knowledge. The line graphs in this chapter express class-inclusion relations, conditional relations, and relations of ranking or rating according to value. The language to express the meaning of the graphs is part of Leech and Svartvik's first type, the conceptual aspect of communication. (An exception is the language of evaluation.) The language for the discussion of a graph includes ways of giving and eliciting information, expressions of possibility and certainty, and suggestions and advice. Relevant here are Leech and Svartvik's second and third types of meaning: the logical and interactional aspects of communication. The language for connected discourse about a graph relates to the fourth type of meaning, the organizational aspect of communication.

The learner converting a graphic into connected discourse thus expresses the conceptual meaning of the graph and adds to this the logical, interactional, and organizational aspects of communication. Leech and Svartvik's type of meaning is based on Halliday's analysis of language into three major components, the ideational, the interpersonal and the textual (Halliday and Hasan, 1976:26–7). Consequently, Halliday's analysis is likely to be the most fruitful approach for future research which compares formal graphic representations of meaning with discourse in natural language.

4.6 SUMMARY
AND CONCLUSION

Without some background knowledge, none of us can adequately interpret or understand individual occurrences. Without background knowledge of the relationship between temperature and water, we cannot understand why a puddle freezes in winter; we cannot interpret an individual increase or decrease in the interest rate without knowledge about the demand for credit; nor can we fully appreciate Shakespeare's *Hamlet* without background knowledge of dramatic conventions.

In this chapter, using the example of teaching a unit on nutrition, we have explored how background knowledge can be presented. Background knowledge is the general, theoretical aspect of an activity, and contains classification, principles, and evaluation. In the example, it was shown how these three knowledge structures can be keyed to their associated thinking processes, communicated through graphics, and related to language items that can be used in the classroom.

For each knowledge structure, appropriate thinking processes were identified. Thus classification includes the thinking processes of comparing and grouping or classifying. A cause and effect principle (just one of the many principles that can be taught) includes inferring, predicting, formulating hypotheses, and generalizing about a cause-effect relationship. Evaluation includes rating and ranking according to some criterion or standard, and deciding among possible alternatives.

Classification, principles, and evaluation were represented by tables and line graphs. It can easily be seen how this approach can be generalized to many other aspects of academic knowledge where relations can be represented by graphic and symbolic forms.

Classification, principles, and evaluation are also structures of semantic relations, and line graphs represent these semantic relations. Notional or semantic grammars of English simply list ways these semantic relations are expressed in English. In addition, these grammars specify the logical, interactional, and organizational aspects of communication that are needed to talk and write about classification, principles, and evaluation. Learning to talk and write about these knowledge structures is then an important part of the development of competence in academic language.

However, in exploring ways in which we can use graphics to develop the learner's thinking processes and language competency, our goal is much broader. Classification, principles, and evaluation are fundamental to knowledge. In the nutrition unit, students are not only learning to classify food, they are learning the structure of classification. They are learning about grouping, class-inclusion, and class-exclusion when classifying food items, just as they are learning about conditional relations and rating and ranking in other parts of the unit. Therefore, by recognizing and using the knowledge structures of an activity, the content teacher and the language teacher can develop a common approach in teaching for a transfer of thinking skills across the curriculum.

EXERCISES FOR CHAPTER FOUR

1. Pick a knowledge structure from the kinds mentioned in the chapter (classification, principles, evaluation). Think of various different ways it might show up in your students' experiences, whether as a structure or as the core of a thinking process. Consider any reading, writing, speaking, and listening tasks and also any other kind of work or academic task. Then list some examples to show the variety of different ways it shows up.

   e.g. Classification
   - paragraphs of classification
   - the contents page of a book
   - book structure generally, such as the encyclopedia as a classification of knowledge
   - the classification of parts of a newspaper such as the opinion page or the international news section
   - library classifications as reflected in the card indexes in libraries
   - files in business
   - sorting plants and animals into classes in botany and biology
   - classification of subject area concepts in other content areas.

2. Look at any textbook for first or second language learners. Find a knowledge structure like the kinds mentioned in this chapter. Describe how the textbook makes use of the knowledge structure. Consider, where appropriate, any of the issues in the second section of the chapter: the data presented to the students, student activities, and how the knowledge structure is related to aspects of language.

3. Apply exercise 2 to two different subject areas. Compare the examples of the knowledge structure in the two areas. Discuss how you would use the examples to teach for transfer of thinking skills and language from one subject area to another.

4. Apply exercise 2 to two language textbooks with different approaches to language teaching. Compare the way the knowledge structure is used in the two approaches. For example, you could compare how classification is handled in two ESL textbooks, such as Robert Bander, *American English Rhetoric* (a models and manipulation approach) and Mary Lawrence, *Writing as a Thinking Process* (a writing as thinking approach).

5. Look at any content course that stresses inquiry skills, thinking processes, or discovery learning. Suggest ways you could use a table, diagram, or other graphic to highlight the structure of knowledge related to one of these thinking processes and to guide the thinking process. Or, if a graphic is already being used, discuss whether you could use it more effectively for these purposes.

6. Find a textbook on research methods, philosophy of science, educational evaluation, ethics and value theory, decision making, or statistics. University level textbooks are the most obvious choice, such as R. Giere, *Understanding Scientific Reasoning*. Look for an

idea relating to classification, principles, and evaluation (e.g., hypotheses, cause, correlation). Discuss it, giving some examples. It may be helpful if you can find a definition of the idea, and if you can find a table or diagram that illustrates it.

This is an advanced exercise, aimed at getting a clear idea of a very general knowledge structure for your own purposes. Getting a bit clearer about a general idea will be a help in seeing the different ways it shows up in thinking processes in the classroom.

7. Search textbooks, newspapers for a graphic and some text that goes with it. For example, the business section of the newspaper may have an article on unemployment and a table of unemployment figures. Discuss how the graphic and the text are related—the text may summarize the table and discuss its implications, for instance. Is the text really necessary or could the reader get all necessary information from the graphic? What semantic relations appear in both the table and the text?

8. Find subject area curricula that list thinking processes. Use Figure 4.21 to select thinking processes that relate to classification, principles, and evaluation. Demonstrate that these are cross-content thinking processes.

9. Choose classification or principles or evaluation. Examine content area materials and language teaching materials where the knowledge structure appears. Make a list of the language items used to express the knowledge structure.

CHAPTER FOUR
SUGGESTED READINGS

Bruner, J. et al. 1970. *Man: A Course of Study*. Washington, D.C.: Curriculum Development Associates. A social sciences and humanities curriculum designed for students in the elementary school, covering language, tool use, social organization, mythology, and the biological nature of humans. Emphasizes the scientific mode of observation, speculation, hypothesis making and testing, understanding of particular social science disciplines, and discovery learning.

Cooper, J. 1979. *Think and Link*. London: Edward Arnold. A course for advanced ESL students to read and write English through the presentation and practice of the ways in which ideas and information are organized in English. Deals with sequencing, classification, comparison, and contrast using exercises such as filling in tables, charts, graphs, marking routes on a map, and labelling and drawing diagrams.

Giere, R. 1979. *Understanding Scientific Reasoning*. New York: Holt, Rinehart and Winston. A university level text to help beginning philosophy, science, and business students to evaluate and utilize scientific information. Deals with theories; causes, correlations and statistical reasoning; values and decisions. Explains these clearly.

Lawrence, M. 1975. *Reading, Thinking, Writing*. Ann Arbor: University of Michigan Press. A text combining reading, writing, and thinking for students of English as a second language who are still mastering basic grammatical patterns. The lessons capitalize on the student's natural ability to think inductively, to draw inferences, to manipulate data, and to make syntheses. Based on the ideas of Jerome Bruner, the book provides practice in chronological order, description, generalization plus examples, comparison and contrast, cause and effect, and hypothesis.

McKim, R. 1980. *Experiences in Visual Thinking*. (2nd ed.). Monterey, California: Brooks/Cole. Visual thinking describes the interaction between seeing, imagining, and idea-sketching. McKim discusses the nature of visual thinking, the kinds of visual imagery that are primary vehicles of visual thinking, and how visual thinking involves many kinds of active operations. One chapter deals with ways in which visual thinking provides an important creative complement to modes of thinking such as verbal thinking.

McNeil, J. 1981. *Curriculum*. (2nd ed.) Boston: Little, Brown. Chapter 4, "The Academic Subject Curriculum," outlines the structure of knowledge approach to curriculum development and relates it to the history of recent developments in curriculum. The structure of knowledge approach organizes materials around the primary structural elements of a discipline: key concepts, principles, and modes of enquiry. Teaching materials in this approach usually contain lists of thinking skills.

Meredith, P. 1961. *Learning, Remembering and Knowing*. London: The English Universities Press. A simply-written book about how to study independently in the 'Teach Yourself' series. It claims that the key to learning, remembering, and knowing is organization. Contains chapters on the organization of knowledge and on the graphic language of organization.

Merritt, J. et al. 1977. *Developing Independence in Reading*. Milton Keynes: The Open University Press. A course for teachers which deals with advanced reading skills relating to the organization of meanings that we may derive from print to satisfy our various reading purposes. Shows with numerous examples how comprehension can often be illustrated by a drawing, a graph, a table, a network, or some other model. These models can be used to record information for reference or to present information to others.

Stubbs, M. 1980. *Language and Literacy: the Sociolinguistics of Reading and Writing*. London: Routledge and Kegan Paul. The study of literacy is still a very confused topic which requires the integration of findings from different areas. Stubbs argues that reading and writing are psychological skills, but they are also linguistic skills (since people read and write meaningful language), and social skills (since written language serves particular functions in different societies).

Whitman, M. 1981. *Writing: the Nature, Development and Teaching of Written Communication*. *Vol. 1*. Hillsdale, N. J.: Erlbaum . A recent collection of papers on a broad range of aspects of writing. See, for example, the paper by Cook-Gumperz and Gumperz entitled "From Oral to Written Culture: the Transition to Literacy."

Widdowson, H. (ed.). 1979. *Reading and Thinking in English*. Oxford: Oxford University Press. A course in reading comprehension for students of English as a foreign language, in a series of four books ranging from near beginner to advanced. Prepares the student for the specialist English met in textbooks without being biased towards any one subject. It deals with communicative functions common in academic writing, such as generalizing, describing, defining, classifying, and hypothesizing.

Chapter 5

From Practical
to Theoretical

5.1 INTRODUCTION

Every teacher organizes learning experiences so that students can build on initial understandings and progress from the easy to the more difficult, providing a sequence of learning and development. This raises the question of how the development of language learning can be coordinated with the development of content learning. How can learning experiences be organized to help both language learning and content learning? Content courses must address this question because they are taught through the medium of language. Less obviously, language courses must address the same question because they almost always follow some sequence of content topics.

In the last three chapters we have shown the usefulness of the knowledge framework in promoting communication, thinking, and language across the curriculum. Chapter 2 presented the knowledge framework based on activities, and Chapters 3 and 4 discussed the practical side of an activity (the action situation) and the theoretical side (background knowledge) in greater detail, giving examples of how they can be applied in the classroom.

This chapter examines the transition from the practical aspect to the theoretical aspect of activities. It examines the transition from particular action situations to background knowledge, showing that the knowledge framework also provides useful general guidelines for curriculum design.

The aim here, then, is to arrive at some broad general principles for the joint sequencing of language learning and content learning. In turn, the goal for these principles should be to enable the development of language learning and the development of content learning to be mutually supportive.

5.2 SEQUENCING LANGUAGE EXPERIENCES

In several different ways language teachers face the issue of how to sequence language experiences. They plan the sequence of the language course; they decide how to develop a unit plan; they are asked to advise on which content courses second language learners should begin with and which ones are best left till later; they judge which language contact situations learners are likely to find easy and which ones are likely to be difficult. From their experience with language learners, they build up a sense of which communication situations are comfortable for the beginner and which communication situations are more suitable for the advanced learner.

A major aspect of first or second language development is an increasing ability to make meaning explicit, to communicate ideas through words alone. The learner develops an increasing ability to interpret discourse and an increasing ability to express experience and understanding in discourse. This is highly relevant to school learning since, as James Moffett puts it, "rendering experience into words is the real business of the schools." An important question is the direction taken by this development.

In teaching or learning anything it is usually a good idea to start from practical example and cases and move towards theoretical understanding, rather than the other way around. Communication with a learner is often easier if you start with the specific and move towards the general. Language learners typically find it less difficult to talk about the "here and now" than to talk about matters which are remote and general. Teachers, and language teachers particularly, are very skilled at using all manner of student experiences, equipment, props, films, visual aids, and the classroom setting itself to build an initial basis for talk about the "here and now." They are also skilled at moving away from the specific towards general implications. This is typically done by drawing attention to contrasting examples, posing problems, raising questions, and encouraging discussion, reflection, speculation, and hypothesis.

Starting from the practical in learning and teaching means going from practical understanding to theoretical understanding and from practical talk (talk about the specific case) to theoretical talk (talk about background knowledge). This happens throughout teaching in general and throughout language teaching in particular. Yet, remarkably, there is very little discussion of it in analyses of language learning and teaching.

The dominant plan for sequencing language courses has been to follow a sequence of sentence patterns and grammar rules. Though this pattern can still be found within many classrooms, it is now widely questioned. In a recent review of sequencing, Stern (1983:395) points out that the accepted practice of grading and sequencing the language input has been challenged. The assumption that an arrangement of the language in carefully graded steps would correspond to the natural learning sequence of language acquisition is disputed. At the same time Stern notes that research on language acquisition does not have definitive answers on which to base an alternative plan. In these circumstances no principle for sequencing language experiences can be offered with any certainty. On the other hand, it is a good moment to take a broader look at the problem to try to find some systematic picture which might guide future work. Many discussions of language sequencing, developmental or otherwise, assume that we need consider language only. Attention is directed at the development of the language system. These discussions do not consider language in context.

Yet there is evidence that discourse about a particular situation (practical discourse) in a familiar context is necessary for beginning language learners. "The available evidence for both child and adult second language learners in a host or foreign language environment suggests that language environments rich in concrete referents appear to be a necessary environmental characteristic for beginning second language learners" (Dulay, Burt, and Krashen, 1982:29). Language directed at beginning language learners must be such that learners can work out the meaning to some extent from the nonlinguistic context. This can be managed by following the "here-and-now" principle of talking about what is immediately present rather than about matters which are distant in time or place.

D'Anglejan (1978) makes a related point about the importance of extralinguistic context, saying that verbal fluency in the second language is most effectively acquired when the learning context is one of informal learning. Informal learning is typical of traditional societies where formal schooling has not emerged as an institution. Hunting, fishing, and farming were learned by observation and direct participation. In informal settings learning takes place in real situations where meaning is evident from the context. In a formal learning setting, as in the classroom, learning is often removed from the context of socially relevant action into an environment of language and symbolic activity.

While context-dependent practical discourse is important for the early stages of language learning, competence in processing relatively context-independent theoretical discourse is necessary for academic achievement and is a major aim of schooling. Cummins (1981, 1983) distinguishes between the processing of language in informal everyday situations and the language processing required in academic situations. There is evidence that within one and a half to two years after arrival in the host country, most immigrant students have acquired relatively fluent face-to-face communication skills in the second language. Yet it takes them about five to seven years on the average to approach grade norms in English cognitive/academic skills, as indicated by tests of vocabulary. "A major pedagogical principle for both L1 and L2 teaching is that language skills in context-reduced situations can be most successfully developed on the basis of initial instruction which maximises the degree of context-embeddedness i.e., clues to meaning" (Cummins, 1983:125). In other words, the learner needs to start from practical discourse and move towards theoretical discourse.

Restating these ideas as principles of sequencing we get: (1) move from experiential learning to expository learning; (2) move from practical content to theoretical content; and (3) move from practical talk to theoretical talk.

From experiential to
expository learning

As we said in Chapter 2, teaching and learning can be divided into experiential approaches and expository approaches. Experiential learning is learning through first-hand
experiences and observation, such as laboratory work, demonstrations, practical
activity in art, music, and home economics, and first-hand contact with data in discovery
learning. Expository learning is learning through discourse, including teaching and
learning by lecture, textbook and classroom discussion. We have discussed how, in
traditional societies, learning is a matter of learning by experience, learning by doing.
It occurs informally and incidentally through practical communication in action situations. The growth of society has meant that much of a child's education is now provided
by formal learning in the classroom. Formal learning is typically expository learning
from texts and teachers, learning intentionally by talk. It often aims at understanding
theoretical concepts through theoretical discourse, and even if it is about action situations it is distant from them.

Dewey (1916:Ch. 1) noted the dangers inherent in the transition from informal
to formal education. In a complex society, much of what has to be learned is stored in
symbols. Formal learning may be bookish and merely verbal, isolated from life experience. As a corrective, Dewey wished to start from the learner's practical experience.
But he also wished to keep a proper balance between the experiential and the expository.
Experiential learning, though personal and vital, is often narrow. Hence the importance
of broadening out from the learner's practical experience and developing the learner's
theoretical understanding.

For Dewey, an important principle of educational growth was to develop from the
experiential and practical to the expository and theoretical:

> When education, under the influence of a scholastic conception of knowledge
> which ignores everything but scientifically formulated facts and truths, fails to
> recognize that the primary or initial subject matter always exists as matter of an
> active doing, involving the use of the body and the handling of material, the subject
> matter of instruction is isolated from the needs and purposes of the learner, and so
> becomes just a something to be memorized and reproduced upon demand (Dewey
> 1916:184).

This suggests the familiar idea of starting with concrete things and moving to
abstract symbols. But Dewey means more than this: not simply starting with objects,
recognizing and labelling them, but starting with a beginning understanding of objects
in the functional context of an activity; not simply recognizing and labelling a pawn in
chess, but seeing it as a piece in a game. Moreover "active doing" is an interplay between
the world and the purposes and understandings of the learner, for Dewey sees the
human being as a problem-solver, putting experience to the question. Further, physical
doing is a starting point and not an endpoint:

The positive principle is maintained when the young begin with active occupations having a social origin and use, and proceed to a scientific insight in the material and laws involved, through assimilating into their more direct experience the ideas and facts communicated by others who have had a larger experience (Dewey, 1916:193).

In fact, Dewey sees:

> ... three fairly typical stages in the growth of subject matter in the experience of the learner. In its first estate, knowledge exists as the content of intelligent ability— power to do. This kind of subject matter, or known material, is expressed in familiarity or acquaintance with things. Then this material gradually is surcharged and deepened through communicated knowledge or information. Finally, it is enlarged and worked over into rationally or logically organized material that of one who, relatively speaking, is expert in the subject (Dewey, 1916:184).

The physical aspect of an activity has an importance beyond aiding the mental development of the child, for it is crucial in securing understanding in communication in general. As any teacher who has used the direct method of second language teaching knows, it is an indispensable way of communicating with second language learners of any age. And, for native speakers, it is a security against living in isolated private worlds of meaning, for it is ultimately only by reference to a common spatio-temporal framework of material things that "we can make it clear to each other what or which particular things our discourse is about because we can fit together each other's reports and stories into a single picture of the world" (Strawson, 1959:38).

The growth principle of starting from the learner's practical experience is not unqualified. Moffett (1976:460) has pointed out that the development of figurative discourse, as opposed to literal discourse, seems to work in the reverse direction: from there-then settings and far-fetched characters and actions to the here-now of contemporary realism. Children first project themselves into fairy tales, myths, and legends and are only later willing to recognize the personal meaning symbolized in these myths.

Given this qualification, there are various ways in which the learner's experience can be expanded from the more practical to the more theoretical. One way is to expand from the social environment that the learner is familiar with.

> At first the material is such as lies nearest the child himself, the family life and its neighborhood setting; it then goes on to something slightly more remote, social occupations ... and then extends itself to the historical evolution of typical occupations and of the social forms connected with them (Dewey, 1900:106).

Another way is for the expert to help the learner put experience into words. A description or commentary, and the form it takes in language, may seem perfectly obvious to the expert but it need not be at all obvious to the learner. It is hardly accidental that the best-known way of doing this is called the language-experience approach. A third way is the discovery approach to teaching where the expert takes "pains to see that [the] one learning engages in significant situations where his own activities generate, support and clinch ideas—that is, perceived meanings and connections" (Dewey, 1916:160).

Dewey's view implies that we should build on the transition between the experiential and the expository. This occurs when students follow an experiment, a simulation, or a case study with a discussion or a report, reflecting on their experience. The importance of this for language learning is that it is a transition from discourse interwoven with action and observation to discourse where the message is expressed by words alone.

From practical to theoretical content

Practical content deals with specifics, with knowledge of particular events at a specific time. In chess, this would be knowledge of what is happening in a particular game. By contrast, theoretical content deals with general concepts and provides a background of interpretation for specifics. In chess, this would be knowledge of the rules and strategies which enable us to interpret many different particular games.

Some content curricula show the sequence from practical experience to theoretical understanding on a large scale. Starting in the 1930s, Paul Hanna developed a multi-disciplinary curriculum for social studies in the elementary school. This curriculum was strongly influenced by Dewey's ideas and reflected the growth principle. Hanna's leading concept is the expanding environments or expanding communities plan, which is based on the assumption that learners are initially most interested in and best able to comprehend those things that are close at hand:

> The sequence of themes or emphasis is drawn from the fact that each of us lives within a system or set of expanding communities that starts with the oldest, smallest and most crucial community—the family placed in the center of concentric circles—and progresses outward in every widening bands . . . . (Hanna et al. 1970:3).

In sequence these are:

1. the child's family community

2. the child's school

3. the child's neighborhood community

4. the child's local communities: country, city, county, metropolis

5. the child's state community

6. the child's region of states community

7. the United States national community

Over this set of expanding communities of people, Hanna lays a grid of clusters of human activities; the basic human activities in each community are divided under nine headings:

1. protecting and conserving life and resources

2. producing, exchanging, and consuming goods and services

3. transporting goods and people

4. communicating facts, ideas, and feelings

5. providing education

6. providing recreation

7. organizing and governing

8. expressing esthetic and spiritual impulses

9. creating new tools, techniques, and institutions

The development of an item within Hanna's total design can be illustrated by the way the concept of social rules is introduced in the first grade. Initially, a story might be presented dealing with a classroom incident where a student challenges a teacher about a rule that *you must sit down when others are working*. The students discuss the story and the teacher guides the discussion towards the principle that a democratic group permits its members to discuss its social rules and possibly change them. The development is therefore from practical experience to theoretical principle.

The expanding environments design encourages the development from experiential learning towards a greater degree of expository learning. The design begins with material which is familiar and close to the learner. This offers opportunities for action, observation, and experiential learning, such as visits to the local community. The design expands to material which is distant from the learner and must often be communicated through discourse. Here expository learning must play a larger role.

In various shapes and forms something rather similar to the expanding environments plan of content underlies a number of second language courses. It is difficult for a language course to exclude *all* content. The question is whether the content is selected at random, or whether there is some systematic planning of the content progression. Some ESL teachers in elementary school use a progression rather like Hanna's. They begin with the the learner in the classroom, deal with the school (its layout and personnel), and then discuss the learner's journey to school, the learner's family, the local neighborhood. Even second language courses which are mainly designed around a progression of sentence structures often reveal a similar but hidden content plan. For example, *Steps to English Book 1*, which is part of an ESL text series for elementary students, describes the following sequence of topics through dialogues and stories: the students, the classroom and the school, the family at home, the grocery store, the bus, the shoe store, the local neighborhood, the swimming pool, the fire department, the post office, the doctor's office (Kernan, 1974).

There are ESL courses which are explicitly based on themes and designed around a content progression. Corder describes a projected theme-based course where, as in the expanding environments design, the logic of sequencing "usually follows some sort of progression from the more familiar situation, the home, the school, to the less familiar area of experience, the airport, the hotel, etc." (Corder, 1973:320). Where Hanna divides basic human activities into nine headings, this course divides the world into four basic areas of activity and interest:

1. personal relationships within the family and among friends

2. social relationships and activities of the community

3. cultural life—habits, customs, traditions, etc.

4. the natural environment, science, technology, etc.

Most second language courses include the goal of teaching the culture of the society that speaks the target language. It is in the area of teaching culture, broadly interpreted, that second language courses and social studies courses approach each other most closely. The second language teacher is faced with the problem of finding an organized body of information about the culture and adapting it for teaching. Clearly the most obvious source for an analysis of the culture and society already organized for teaching is the social studies course for native speakers. Finocchiaro and Bonomo (1973:60) have given a clear and detailed example of a cultural syllabus which can be used as a cultural strand within a second language course. They list nine main headings, each with up to eleven subheadings. Predictably, the main headings follow the expanding environments design; they start with the students, the immediate classroom, and the school, and later move on to the immediate community of the school and home and to the wider community. What is more, within each main heading the subheadings often parallel Hanna's main divisions of human activity. Under the heading of the immediate community, for example, we have the subheadings of homes, consumer services (stores, banks etc.), transportation facilities (directions, tickets), communication facilities (telephone, mail, newspaper), education facilities and so on.

The second language teacher and the social studies teacher face a similar problem of developing an understanding of a culture and society. Therefore, it is no surprise that they arrive at similar solutions. Clearly the tradition of teaching social studies has had a strong and generally unacknowledged influence on the teaching of culture by the language teacher. More than this though, the systematic planning of the expanding content progression of a second language course is organized that way not only for reasons of content but also for reasons of language.

The expanding environments plan parallels a traditional language teaching principle that language teaching must be situational. If the learner doesn't know the second language, how does the teacher communicate with him? The teacher communicates through action situations, where the circumstances make the meanings clear. Both expanding environments and situational language teaching start with the familiar and close at hand. But situational language teaching begins even more concretely with active doing involving the use of the body and the handling of material because of the problem of communicating with the learner:

We are making a village with cardboard houses and paper trees in the first few weeks of learning the language; a boy wants more sticky paper to stick the walls of his house together. He hesitates and looks at the sticky paper in the teacher's hand. 'May I have some sticky paper, please?' whispers the teacher in his ear. 'May I have some sticky paper, please?' he repeats urgently, reaching for the roll . . . (Billows, 1961:7).

Here the meaning of the interaction is carried by the learner's situation. The speech is an accompaniment of the action, it is relatively redundant, and it is not the prime mover. Because of this, the speech can be learned incidentally, and not as an overt language learning task. "The repetition of words and word patterns in situations that are perfectly clear brings the language into mind without any effort of comprehension . . . even if no single word is understood at first' (Billows, 1961:5). Starting with familiar situations makes the second language more accessible to the learner. It is highly re-dundant practical talk about practical content.

Of course this does not mean teaching only what we can see and touch. What advocates of situational language teaching have often failed to explain is how the learner's situation can be expanded progressively beyond what is seen and touched. We can see how the progression of topics does this for content, but how is the learner's language expanded? Billows (1961:9–12) divides the situation of the learner into "four con-centric spheres, with the learner at the centre."

1. The first sphere is "what the learner can see, hear, and touch directly, as in the example above. In practice this is the classroom situation . . . ." Here words are merely an accompaniment of action.

2. The second is "what the learner knows from his own experience, his daily life, what he has seen and heard directly but cannot see or hear at the moment" (e.g., the home and the neighborhood). This can be brought to mind by the use of words together with the classroom situation.

3. The third is what the learner "has not yet experienced directly, but what he can call to mind with an effort of the imagination, with the help of pictures, dramatization, charts and plans."

4. The fourth is "what is brought into his mind through the spoken, written or printed word alone, without help through audio-visual aids," that is, through textual material.

Thus, the spheres are arranged in order of increasing distance from the familiar "here-and-now," from discourse which is highly context dependent to discourse which is much less context dependent. The ultimate aim is to develop the outer sphere—the ability to handle textual material which conveys unfamiliar information.

Situational language teaching techniques do not mean that the learner is restricted to communicating about what is trivial and obvious, even for the very young learner beginning a second language. Cantieni and Tremblay (1973) describe a K-3 program where English-speaking primary school children learn French and mathematics simultaneously. They develop mathematics learning through the manipulation of concrete materials. Mathematical concepts are taught through the description of physical objects, qualities, and actions. The description of physical objects, qualities, and action is similarly the basis for learning concrete nouns, color adjectives, commands, and spatial prepositions.

To sum up, the expanding environments design expands the learner's ability to understand less familiar and more distant environments; parallelling this, the language teacher expands the ability of the learner to handle discourse which is less and less context dependent. Combining content and language learning, the student then learns about less familiar and more distant content largely through the spoken and written word alone.

From practical to theoretical discourse

Practical discourse is discourse associated with action situations and specific practical knowledge (see Chapter 3); theoretical discourse is discourse associated with general, background knowledge (see Chapter 4). The automobile insurance material in Chapter 2 illustrated the contrast between the two kinds of discourse.

The dialogue in the insurance photostory (Figure 2.2) is an example of practical discourse. It is conversational interaction in an action context: conversation about a particular car crash. Utterances are heavily dependent on their context for their interpretation; it is context dependent discourse. The speaker is face to face with the hearer, feedback is possible, and miscommunication can be corrected. Much is conveyed by the situation and need not be stated.

The newspaper articles about car insurance (Figure 2.3) are examples of theoretical talk. They are relatively context independent discourse. They are written monologues aimed at developing an understanding of the principles of insurance rather than guiding action. The writer is not present to the reader, feedback is not possible, and possible misunderstandings must be detected and corrected in advance. Little is conveyed by the situation, and the text contains much of its meaning within itself. It must spell out and elaborate this meaning explicitly.

Practical discourse is characteristic of everyday interactions in society; theoretical discourse is characteristic of language in school learning—academic discourse.

A language curriculum should contain some plan for sequencing discourse from practical discourse to theoretical discourse.

A standard model for the English language curriculum has two main dimensions: 1) language skills and 2) language components. See Figure 5.1. Various additional language components can be added to this model, such as language notions and language functions.

It would seem that this model is merely commonsense, yet it is important to recognize the assumptions it makes. The model starts from items of language and the

Figure 5.1

A Standard Model of the Language Curriculum

Language Components	Language Skills			
	Listening	Speaking	Reading	Writing
Phonology/ Orthography				
Structure				
Vocabulary				
Rate and general fluency				

Source: Harris (1969:11)

distinction between the spoken mode and the written mode. This is a language-only model which limits itself to the language specialist's point of view. It does not attempt to find common elements between language curricula and content curricula. It is not surprising therefore that it blocks the development of language-content connections. It is a blind alley. An additional model is needed which would reflect the difference between practical, context dependent discourse and theoretical, relatively context independent discourse.

Moffett (1968a) points out that the initial distinction between the spoken mode and the written mode (as in Figure 5.1) leaves us at the superficial level of a distinction between language expressed in sounds and language expressed in marks. It encourages us to think of writing as a mere transcription of speech. It is much more productive to plan a curriculum from a completely different initial basis.

The most comprehensive curriculum design for English language education is presented in Moffett's *Teaching the Universe of Discourse* and *Student-Centered Language Arts and Reading K-13* (Moffett 1968a, 1968b, Moffet and Wagner, 1976). Designed for native speakers from kindergarten to the end of high school, the plan includes both reading and writing, speaking and listening, and is concerned to integrate language arts with other media.

Moffett's approach begins with communication and discourse. He sees the communicative act as a relation between *I*, a speaker or writer, *you*, a listener or reader, and *it*, the material under discussion: *I* indicate something to *you* about *it*. A discourse is

... any complete communication having a sender, receiver, and message bound by a purpose ... e.g. a conversation, a lecture, a letter or journal, poem or short story, ad or label .... A complete discourse is the only language unit worthy of being made a learning unit ... (Moffett and Wagner, 1976:12).

To communicate is to overcome a differential, some imbalance of information between the two parties, an information gap. The learner develops in the ability to communicate successfully across wider and wider information gaps or information distances. This can be compared with the expanding environments design. The "things that make for variation in discourse can be put as a matter of time and space. (1) How large in time and space is the speaker, the listener, the subject? (2) How great is the distance between them?" (Moffett, 1968:32).

One type of information gap or distance is that between the sender and the receiver. This is distance as dissimilarity between people. Discourses can be arranged in order of increasing distance in this sense:

1. reflection

2. conversation

3. correspondence

4. publication

Reflection is intrapersonal communication, the self as both sender and receiver. Distance is at a minimum. At the furthest distance, publication is impersonal communication to a large anonymous group extended over space and time. Unlike conversation and correspondence, feedback is not possible. It is more selective and composed.

A second type of distance is between the sender and the topic. This is distance in the sense of increasing abstraction between raw experience and the verbalization of it. The discourse arrangement for this kind of distance is:

1. drama

2. narrative

3. exposition

4. argumentation

This is in order of increasing abstraction and is a sequence of action dialogue, reporting, generalizing, and theorizing.

The total curriculum is essentially an arrangement of different forms of discourse, from the least distant to the most distant, along both dimensions of distance. So, for instance, at the kindergarten to third grade level some of the forms of discourse practiced are: acting out stories, show and tell, writing captions, informal discussions. Some at the tenth to thirteenth grade level are: interviews, reportage, research, generalization, and theory. Show and tell, such as a boy showing his classmates a shell he collected from the beach, is face-to-face and conversational, and somewhere between drama and narrative. By contrast, a research report written for a general audience would be between correspondence and publication, and involve exposition and argumentation.

Figure 5.2 shows schematically the two dimensions of distance in combination. Show and tell is at the near end (where the distances on both dimensions are small),

Figure 5.2

Two kinds of distance combined:

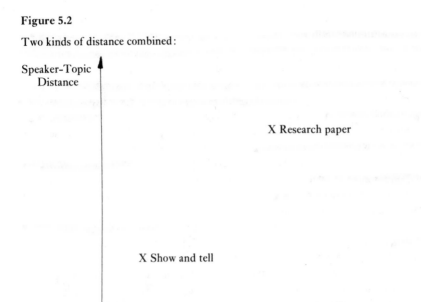

and the research paper is at the far end (where the distances are relatively great). Taken together, the two dimensions of discourse show the direction of the learner's growth in discourse. Two qualifications are necessary, however. We are speaking particularly of literal discourse. Figurative or imaginative discourse works rather differently. As we noted earlier, learners may show an early interest in far-off myths and legends and only later appreciate stories close to their own situation. Secondly, the direction of growth works in a general way only:

> Younger learners will find later discourse areas hard to work in, but even primary children may practice language in all . . . areas concurrently, either by speaking some kinds before they can write them, or reading them before they can speak them, or by sending and receiving very short instead of long continuities (Moffett and Wagner, 1976:457).

The contrast between show and tell and the research paper also shows a sequence of growth "from mixing various kinds of discourse within dialogue to singling out each kind of discourse separately in monologue" (Moffett and Wagner, 1976:455). While show and tell is a short informal chat, blending fact and opinion, fun and seriousness, the research paper, like other forms of academic discourse, is a sustained attempt at a specific purpose. It must be relevant, marshall evidence for claims made, and be clearly differentiated from other forms of discourse like imaginative fiction.

One way Moffett's plan for discourse development can be implemented in the language classroom is by arranging for peer teaching and peer communication about topics of interest. He aims to develop the learner's communicative competence. By changing the traditional teaching approach (which provides information about language and treats language in isolation), Moffett wants to encourage natural occasions for language use by students and arrange for realistic communication situations. The discourse is expected to become increasingly complex as the distance is increased.

Moffett points out that the typical arrangements of the language classroom undermine this aim in three ways. In the typical language classroom work is standardized so that every individual does the same thing. Consequently, an individual learner has little new information to convey to any other individual. Second, the communication pattern of the classroom is such that the individual learners communicate with the teacher but not with each other. The teacher becomes a communication bottleneck. Third, language is compartmentalized from other subject areas and becomes isolated from its natural purpose. It becomes a thing by itself.

Moffett's remedies for this situation are the three I's: *individualization, interaction*, and *integration*. With *individualization*, the individual is given power to choose his own activities and materials. One of the results of this is that the learner has something to say. *Interaction* entails arranging for the students to center on and teach each other. *Integration* essentially means the integration of language arts with other arts and media and with other subject areas. Moffett and Wagner (1976: Chapter 2) make an excellent case for these remedies, and details of suggested methods are elaborated throughout the book.

5.3 RELATIONS AMONG DISCOURSE, CONTENT, AND LEARNING

We have discussed the sequencing of learning, content, and discourse in both language and content courses. However, although we treated learning, content, and discourse separately, they are obviously connected. Their central connection can be seen in the explanation of an activity to a learner: the speaker makes understandings about the activity explicit in discourse.

Cazden (1972:185 ff) gives a clear review of theory and research about the development of explicitness in discourse.

> A spot on the rug can be: *it, the spot, the spot near the table*, etc. One source of variation within child language comes from the selection among options for making meaning less or more explicit. One dimension of language development is increasing ability to free language from its nonlinguistic context and communicate ideas through words alone. This has been termed 'coding ability'.

Coding ability depends on two characteristics of the communication: "the presence or absence of a physically present nonlinguistic context and the presence or absence of a shared 'psychological context' of previously acquired information and experience." Coding ability is therefore taxed:

. . . whenever the topic of conversation is not physically present and supplementary nonverbal communication such as pointing is impossible. Familiar occasions include describing the past, planning for the future, giving directions to strangers, talking over the telephone, and writing . . . . In written language, where no physical context is possible, the presence or absence of a shared psychological background becomes all the more important.

An important aspect of coding ability is "skill in adapting one's message to the listener or reader. This may require the recognition of differences in either perceptual or conceptual points of view." In other words, information gaps in the physical or psychological context tax coding ability and the communicator must recognize these gaps and adapt the message by adding relevant information, producing more explicit speech or more explicit writing. Demanding coding tasks are difficult for all learners. One expects that young native speakers will experience particular difficulty with the cognitive aspect of adapting their messages to an audience. Second language learners will probably find particular difficulty with the linguistic demands of more explicit discourse.

Thus, we can picture this aspect of language development as a progression by the learner through a series of communication situations where the meaning is made increasingly explicit in discourse.

Now consider the child learning about the world. Understanding develops from the immediate, specific, and practical to the distant, general, and theoretical "through assimilating into more direct experience the ideas and facts communicated by others who have had a larger experience" (Dewey, 1916:193). This communication will make explicit those meanings which are hidden in the child's immediate world. The child increases its understanding of the world through communication that makes meanings increasingly explicit. There is therefore a relationship between the development of understanding and language development in terms of explicitness.

This can be seen more clearly if we look at the relation of discourse and knowledge within an activity. An activity gives us something to be explicit about. An activity offers a nonlinguistic context of practical and theoretical knowledge which can be made explicit in discourse. Within an activity, a learner can move from a practical situation in which the meaning is implicit, to theoretical discourse in which the meaning is spelled out for the learner.

In practical situations such as a medical team operating on a patient, scientists conducting an experiment, or a group of workers doing a job, knowledge of the activity is assumed rather than discussed. These are situations of cooperative action between experts who are face-to-face, usually in a physical setting of objects and actions, and nonverbal communication is possible. There is much relevant mutual knowledge, but in these circumstances, it is not normally made explicit in discourse.

The way in which we communicate when we make knowledge explicit depends upon the level of knowledge held (learners or experts), and on the type of knowledge (practical or theoretical). Depending upon whether the participants are knowledgeable about the activity (experts) or not (learners), we make knowledge explicit in different

Figure 5.3

Explicitness in Discourse about an Activity

	Practical understanding explicit	Theoretical understanding explicit
(a) Expert to Expert	Narrative	Theoretical argument
(b) Expert to Learner	Commentary	Exposition

ways: through narrative, theoretical argument, commentary, or exposition. This is illustrated in Figure 5.3.

Suppose we have two people who are competent, expert participants in the activity (a in Figure 5.3). The characters in the earlier car insurance strip story would be an example. Their practical understanding would be made explicit in discourse if one of them narrated the story of what happened to another expert. Their background theoretical understanding would become explicit if they disagreed about their interpretation of the law, and they entered into a theoretical argument. They might even consult statements of the law and insurance. With any activity, then, expert participants can narrate or describe the situation to an expert who is removed from it, and thereby make practical understanding explicit. Or, they can discuss and argue about theoretical understandings, and thereby make theoretical understandings explicit.

On the other hand, suppose an expert is teaching a learner about an activity (b in Figure 5.3). An expert speaking to a learner will not be able to assume the level of understanding that another expert would have. The learner can observe a practical situation, just as students looked at the car insurance action strip. But a learner, unlike an expert, cannot necessarily interpret what is happening. In itself, the physical setting is not enough. The expert may provide a commentary on events, making practical understanding explicit in discourse. Moreover, the learner can not be expected to have the general background of the activity. The expert can provide this through exposition of general principles, making theoretical understanding explicit in discourse. Of course, the learner could elicit this commentary or exposition from an expert by asking questions. Thus, with any activity, a learner can learn from observation of a practical situation, from commentary, and from exposition.

Summarizing Figure 5.3, an expert communicating about an activity with another expert can make practical understanding explicit through narrative and theoretical understanding explicit through theoretical argument. An expert communicating with a learner can make practical understanding explicit through commentary, and theoretical understanding explicit through exposition. Commentary and narrative are practical discourse about an activity; exposition and theoretical argument are theoretical discourse about an activity.

Figure 5.3 hàs direct application to education. Typically, with the teacher as expert and the student as learner, understanding is made explicit through commentary and exposition. Commentary, along with observation and guided participation in practical situations, is usual in experiential approaches to learning. By contrast, exposition includes learning from lectures, seminars, textbooks, and similar forms of expository approaches to learning.

All teachers are aware of the distinction between experiential and expository learning. An important problem, as we have said is managing the transition from experiential to expository learning, keeping in mind both the development of understanding and the development of discourse. This is important if the learner is not to be overwhelmed with language demands. I know of little, if any, research that addresses this problem directly. Teachers manage it in various ways, as when a science teacher gives a demonstration of an experiment, the students repeat the experiment, and a theory lecture follows. We can suggest that commentary and observation help participation in simple practical situations. Commentary on the here-and-now develops the ability to understand narratives of examples more distant in place and time, allowing the topic to be expanded. Exposition of basic principles (as in a textbook) builds a basis for understanding theoretical argument (as in research articles).

Returning to Figure 5.3, the second language learner may be either a learner or an expert. In both cases it is desirable for the student to begin with less explicit discourse in familiar contexts and move to more explicit discourse.

In the content classroom, the second language student is typically a learner of the content topic or activity. In these circumstances the second language learner is likely to be a receiver of different kinds of discourse, from practical to theoretical. The policy of placing the second language learner in classrooms where the content is either practical or familiar is an attempt to provide a gradual development from more practical to more theoretical discourse.

Second language learners can also produce different kinds of discourse as experts in a topic or activity when they have content background. As experts, they can be peer teachers. Arranging the conditions of peer teaching from the practical to the theoretical is then a way to provide for a gradual development from practical to theoretical discourse. This supports the goals of a discourse curriculum in language.

But being a peer teacher is not a possibility for beginning second language learners. They may know the topic or activity but do not have the means to convey this knowledge in the second language. If the language teacher comments on the activity the student is engaged in, the commentary can be a way of presenting the second language to the student. This is situational language teaching at its most basic. The student knows the activity; the commentary deals with familiar ground. For the native speaker it would be highly redundant and pointless discourse. For the second language learner the redundancy is an aid to understanding the new language and producing it. A familiar extralinguistic context is used to interpret unfamiliar language. Again the progression is from language in an action situation, where much is understood nonverbally, towards theoretical discourse, where much is conveyed through language alone.

There is more general agreement among scholars about the nature of practical discourse than about that of theoretical discourse. Therefore, some final remarks about theoretical discourse are in order.

There is no reason to believe that theoretical discourse occurs only in formal educational settings. It may occur in informal learning, too, whenever an expert conveys background knowledge to a learner.

Theoretical discourse is not a social class dialect. Although there is evidence that working–class speakers tend to be less explicit than middle-class speakers (Cazden, 1972:188), and while this might suggest that working-class speakers could find theoretical discourse more difficult to produce, it does necessarily not make theoretical discourse a middle-class variety of language. Theoretical discourse is simply discourse in which theoretical knowledge is made explicit. Failure to recognize this has been largely due to an inadequate model of language, a model which reduces all discourse differences to matters of dialect or style. In fact, it is quite likely that there are different social class styles of theoretical discourse.

Theoretical discourse should not be equated with written discourse alone. It can be spoken as well as written, and it is even likely to be spoken in informal learning settings. It tends to take written form for social and psychological reasons: socially, because it expresses relatively permanent information, as in rules and regulations; psychologically, because the articulation of theory is aided by being able to write it out on the page.

Theoretical discourse is not metalinguistic discourse. It is not discourse about language. It is discourse about an activity. A chemistry textbook is about chemistry. It is theoretical discourse about chemistry. It is not an analysis of the language of chemistry.

Finally, is written theoretical discourse completely context-independent? Is it true, as Cazden states, that "if one is writing to an unknown audience, a 'generalized other', all reliance on any shared background of experience is also withdrawn" (1972:199)? This is not true for many cases of theoretical discourse. Theoretical discourse often relies on a shared background of experience. Theoretical discourse written for experts often requires expert understanding. Advanced reading in subject areas usually requires an advanced understanding of the subject area. Scientific research papers give precise explanations that may not be understandable to the general public. Legal statutes are explicit, but they may need a lawyer to interpret them. Similarly, theoretical discourse written for beginners relies on familiar everyday understanding. Indeed there are those who believe, like Dewey, that understanding can never be transmitted or conveyed to a learner. It can only come about when the learner assimilates new information to his current knowledge through his own efforts. On this view, successful exposition must rely on the learner's experience and practical understanding.

This is not to say that theoretical discourse is limited and controlled by practical understanding. It goes beyond practical understanding, presents possibilities not previously experienced, and restructures practical understanding. It is through the development of theoretical understanding that education can be, as Dewey says, that reconstruction or reorganization of experience which adds to the meaning of experience and which increases ability to direct the course of subsequent experiences. Thus Dearden (1968:125) points out that theoretical concepts may overturn everyday intuitions and make the familiar strange, as with the theoretical concept of light, where there is a change from the everyday concept to that which is invisible and travels. Dewey's concept of growth does not promote the practical over the theoretical.

> But finding the material for learning within experience is only the first step. The next step is the progressive development of what is already experienced into a fuller and richer and also more organized form, a form that gradually approximates that in which subject matter is present to the skilled mature person (Dewey 1938:74). 74).

Practical discourse in practical situations is helpful for Dewey's first step; theoretical discourse for theoretical understanding is essential for the next. Dewey's concept of growth, therefore, leads to an integrated prospective which connects the three sequencing principles of learning, content, and discourse.

5.4 SUMMARY
AND CONCLUSION

Most language teachers are familiar with those language courses which are designed as a sequence of language teaching points, such as a list of grammar rules. Little confidence can be held in this approach to sequencing, since it ignores the fact that language courses contain elements other than language items: students receive and produce discourse; the discourse deals with content topics; and students learn new information about the content topic. In many cases, little thought has been given to sequencing these elements. Yet they are important aspects of language experiences.

The central concern of this chapter was the way in which language experiences can be sequenced in order that the development of language learning can be coordinated with the development of content learning. Linking and expanding on evidence from diverse research sources, I suggest three related principles of sequencing.

1. The sequencing principle for discourse is to move from practical discourse to theoretical discourse. For beginners, this means starting with situational language teaching which relies on the learner's immediate context to make language understandable. Expanding upon situational language teaching, Moffett's discourse curriculum provides suggestions for planning discourse development that eventually leads to written, academic, theoretical, discourse.

2. The sequencing principle for content is to move from practical content to theoretical content. Most language courses have some series of content topics, but the sequence may not always be well chosen, and the topics may be trivial. However, when the language teacher plans the topic sequence for language courses, well-designed content courses are useful examples to follow. The expanding environments plan is an example of content organized from the practical to the theoretical, and it can be seen

that a similar sequence of content topics underlies various second language courses. If we want learners to work with practical discourse, we should choose practical content to talk about. Then, planning a sequence of content from the practical to theoretical will provide the basis for the development of practical to theoretical discourse.

3. The sequencing principle for learning is to move from experiential learning to expository learning. In many language courses, students are, in fact, learning new content information. However, less advanced students are likely to have difficulty learning through expository approaches (such as lectures and textbooks), since expository learning relies on a knowledge of the language. Student and teacher will find it easier to communicate through experiential approaches, such as demonstrations and practical tasks. Moreover, less advanced students will find it easier to communicate with each other in practical tasks; group work like building a model often produces a great deal of communicative interaction.

Peer teaching should also be experiential, at the early stages, since experiential peer teaching and group work give practice in practical discourse. Demonstrating a computer program to another student would be an example in which students would gain practice in practical discourse. For more advanced students, expository peer teaching, such as presenting a written report to class, provides practice in theoretical discourse.

These three related principles of sequencing reflect and extend the work of Dewey in the field of educational philosophy; Hanna in social studies; Billows in second language teaching; and Moffett in first language teaching. Dewey saw intellectual growth in the child as development from experiential learning to expository learning and from practical understanding to theoretical understanding. Hanna's expanding environments design develops from familiar, local, and specific content information to unfamiliar, remote, and general information. Billows' four concentric spheres were aimed at expanding the ability of the learner to handle discourse that is less and less context-dependent. Moffett's curriculum was essentially a development from practical discourse to theoretical discourse, from more implicit to more explicit forms of discourse.

The three related principles of sequence suggested here can be contrasted with those second language curricula which view language development as grammatical development. I suggest a more adequate second language curriculum would include these three principles.

Though we have focused on sequencing in the language class, it must be remembered that the content teacher must also make decisions about sequencing language experiences. The content teacher also wants to avoid language demands which are too difficult for second language learners and wants to help students to improve their ability to communicate.

We have seen that the content course shares common elements with the language course: students produce and receive discourse; the discourse deals with content topics; and students learn new information. The same principles of sequencing apply. To communicate more easily with the students, the content teacher frequently uses more experiential methods and sequences content from the more practical to the more theoretical. To help students improve in communicative ability, the teacher arranges for them to communicate as much as possible. Practical tasks allow students to demonstrate what they know and to engage in practical discourse. Once students have built up a knowledge of a topic, they have something to talk about. They are then in a position to engage in theoretical discourse.

For content teachers of second language learners, the sequence of discourse development, from practical to theoretical, will aid their communication about content material. For language teachers of second language learners, the sequence of content development, from practical to theoretical, will help their students develop a progressive ability in theoretical discourse.

Thus, discourse development and content development can mutually support each other. The three sequencing principles allow the development of language learning and the development of content learning to be coordinated, as the sequencing principles apply to both language courses and content courses for second language learners. In fact, the principles apply very widely across education.

EXERCISES FOR
CHAPTER FIVE

1. Find a second language textbook which follows a sequence of sentence structures but which also follows a sequence of topics (one example is Kernan, *Steps to English*). Often each lesson or unit will have a separate topic. List some of the topics early in the course. List some topics late in the course. Can you see any differences between the early topics and the later topics? Are the earlier topics more specific, familiar, or concrete? For example, in beginning lessons you may find that people are introduced, objects are labelled and scenes are described. The point of this exercise is to see if the textbook uses any principles for organizing topic information and student activity which go beyond teaching a sequence of sentence structures.

2. Choose a second language textbook and look at the topics covered (as in exercise 1 above). Select a topic which is practical, specific, concrete. Select another topic which is more theoretical, general, and abstract. Contrast the language used with each topic, and describe the differences.

3. The chapter lists some of Moffett's least distant forms of discourse (acting out stories, show and tell, writing captions, informal discussions) and some of his more distant forms of discourse (interviews, reportage and research, generalization, and theory). Think of some of the forms of discourse your students engage in. List some that are less distant and some that are more distant. Discuss whether they seem to find the less distant ones easier to deal with.

4. Some content teachers say that second language students do well in the practical aspects of their content course but find it difficult to handle the more academic, verbal, and theoretical parts of the course. Do you know of any examples like this? Do you feel it is true? Do you think problems with the more academic aspects of a course are due to difficulties with language or difficulties with theoretical understanding?

5. List some ways you might arrange for peer teaching by second language learners in the second language. Sometimes student hobbies can be a resource. For example a student

who is a guitarist can demonstrate guitar-playing and discuss some technical background. Another avenue is when the teacher teaches something and the students teach it to someone else. One teacher taught her second language learners to use a word-processing program on the microcomputer and then arranged for them to show first language students how to use it.

6. Find a manual or set of instructions that gives background information for some activity. Arrange for a student to read it and then to act as a peer teacher or resource person for another student engaging in the activity. Examples might be: a student reads the instructions for using a microscope and helps another student to operate the microscope; a student reads the instruction booklet for operating a radio or tape recorder and helps another student to operate it; a student reads a first-aid manual and applies it to a simulated first-aid situation. Manuals are examples of relatively context independent language. The exercise gives practice in applying context independent language and information to a specific practical situation.

7. Content courses and textbooks provide many examples of ways of relating the general to the specific. One science textbook discusses general principles of glaciation and then provides a picture of a glacier as a basis for a review and discussion. A history course may ask a student to imagine he or she is a person at some time in history and to write a journal. Legal concepts can be worked through by role playing a case. Review content material, write a list of similar techniques of making information specific and concrete, and discuss which ones might be suitable for your students.

8. Choose a content textbook. Find a topic that contains a specific example and its background general principles. Contrast the language used to present the example with the language used to present the general principles, and describe the differences.

9. Observe second language students in a situation of context dependent discourse and in a situation of context independent discourse. For instance, you might contrast their language activities in the playground or while socializing with their language activities in the library. Describe some of the language differences you see. You could consider differences in grammar and language function, spoken vs. written language, short discourse vs. long discourse, whether the language use is group or individual, social or intellectual.

10. Review ways to develop theoretical discourse. Language teachers are familiar with various ways of developing language from student experiences. Teachers may arrange a discussion of a community visit, a field trip, or an experiment. An interesting event can be the basis for the daily class journal. Discuss ways in which students can be encouraged to go beyond describing or commenting on the experience to explaining or generalizing about it.

11. Choose any practical situation. The practical situation can be any data that students can comment on and interpret, such as a case study. Have your students develop the theoretical implications of the information. Their conclusions about the data could be written up as a report. Record the language used to discuss the data and comment on how the theoretical implications are expressed.

CHAPTER FIVE
SUGGESTED READINGS

Billows, F. 1961. *The Techniques of Language Teaching*. London: Longman. A practical, readable book on second language teaching. Chapter 1, "Situational Language Teaching," gives a clear, commonsense account of the situational approach to language development, going well beyond the use of the physical context of the classroom.

Bruner, J. 1975. "Language as an Instrument of Thought." In A. Davies (ed.). *Problems of Language and Learning*. London: Heinemann. Bruner suggests that the mere ability to speak a language has little effect on thought processes. Thought processes are transformed only when language use involves "context-free elaboration." Accordingly, he distinguishes between "communicative competence," being able to make utterances which are appropriate to their context, and "analytic competence," the lengthy operation of thinking on text alone. Schools require "analytic competence."

Corder, S. 1973. *Introducing Applied Linguistics*. Harmondsworth, Middlesex: Penguin Books. Chapter 12, "Organisation: The Structure of the Syllabus," discusses the sequencing of sentence structures, lexical items, themes, and skills.

Cummins, J. 1983. "Language Proficiency and Academic Achievement." In J. Oller (ed.). 1983. *Issues in Language Testing Reaserch*. Rowley, Mass.: Newbury House. Discusses the important questions of how language proficiency is related to academic achievement and points out the lack of a clear idea of the nature of language proficiency. Offers a theoretical framework which throws light on the differences between the linguistic demands of the school and those of inter-personal contexts outside the school.

Gerbrandt, G. 1974. *An Idea Book for Acting Out and Writing Language K-8*. Urbana, Ill: National Council of Teachers of English. A practical book of student activities, strongly influenced by the ideas of James Moffett.

Mackey, W. 1965. *Language Teaching Analysis*. London: Longman. Chapter 7, "Gradation," reviews traditional work in sequencing or gradation in the second language curriculum.

McNeil, J. 1981. *Curriculum*. (2nd ed.). Boston: Little, Brown. Chapter 9, "Principles of Curriculum Organisation," contains a review of sequencing, or 'principles of vertical organisation,' as they apply to all areas of the curriculum.

Moffett, J. 1968. *Teaching the Universe of Discourse*. Boston: Houghton Mifflin. A theoretical statement of the rationale for Moffett's Student-centered Language Arts Curriculum, K-13. Takes the view that a course of language learning is a course in thinking, and that the course goal is for the student to become capable of producing and receiving an increasingly broad range of kinds of discourse and ways of thinking. The sequence to this goal is a growth scale going from the personal to the impersonal, from low to high abstraction, from undifferentiated to finely differentiated modes of discourse.

Stern, H. 1983. *Fundamental Concepts of Language Teaching*. Oxford: Oxford University Press. Chapter 18, "Conditions of Learning and the Learning Process," places the question of sequencing the second language curriculum in the context of recent research on the developmental process of language learning.

Chapter 6

Where Language and Content Should Not Be Confused

6.1 INTRODUCTION

For many aspects of language education we have seen that it is beneficial to relate language learning and content learning, rather than to teach language in isolation. We have seen that the language teacher finds that content material offers information of interest and value which students can communicate about. It provides a context for the development of discourse and language. Learning the language of subject areas enables students to gain access to content knowledge and to express this knowledge. And, just as the language teacher gains by considering content, the content teacher gains by considering language. Communication of content material can be improved, thinking skills can be developed more easily, and transfer of learning is enhanced. However, an emphasis on the mutual interests of language teachers and content teachers should not lead us to overlook the distinction between language knowledge and content knowledge. There are aspects of education where the second language learner will be at a disadvantage if this distinction is overlooked.

Testing and evaluation are areas where it is important to distinguish between language knowledge and content knowledge. Everyone is familiar with the distinction between language tests and content tests. Language tests include tests of grammar and tests of reading comprehension, while content tests include achievement tests in areas like biology or economics. It should be apparent that each type of test should only test what it claims to. It should not include, intentionally or otherwise, areas outside its purview. Language tests should test language and content tests should test content. But what seems apparent is not so easy to accomplish in practice: language is intertwined with content.

There is obviously a language factor in content tests, because it is not possible to understand content questions without an understanding of the language they are written in. Suppose you had to take an economics test written in a language unfamiliar to you. It goes without saying that the test would be an invalid test of your knowledge of economics because of the language factor. When students take an achievement test in a language other than their native language, there is a possibility that the language factor will affect the validity of the test.

Is there a content factor in language tests? Do language tests assume nonlinguistic knowledge that second language learners lack? One type of nonlinguistic knowledge is knowledge of the culture of the second language. To what extent are language tests hidden tests of cultural knowledge? To what extent are language tests culturally biased? We will examine the question of cultural bias in reading comprehension tests.

6.2 CULTURAL BIAS IN READING COMPREHENSION TESTS

Cultural differences can lead to differences in interpreting questions in a reading comprehension test. This is true for many second language learners when they lack knowledge of the host culture. In test situations such differences of interpretation become serious difficulties. Some test items in reading comprehension tests require both language knowledge and cultural knowledge. For instance various standardized tests contain such items and thereby discriminate against ESL students. Consider three such problems that reading comprehension tests can pose:

1. Is there cultural bias in reading comprehension tests, and if so, does it matter that there is bias? Would a bias tend to discriminate against certain students?

2. How can teachers and students, the consumers of the tests, identify bias if it exists?

3. Is cultural bias in reading comprehension tests inevitable in principle, or are there systematic ways in which it can be avoided or at least minimized?

To examine these three issues, question items from tests can be analyzed by means of a linguistic approach rather than the more usual statistical one.

Is there cultural bias in reading comprehension tests?

Many people believe that no bias exists in these tests. Robert L. Ebel, a specialist in educational measurement and a past president of the American Educational Research Association, writes:

> Standardized tests of educational achievement have also been attacked for their alleged bias against cultural minorities . . . . How could evidence of bias in a test of educational achievement be produced? To get it one would need a set of biased tests

and a set of unbiased tests of the same achievement. Then if a person or group made consistently lower or higher scores on the biased than on the unbiased tests we would have evidence of bias. But note the problem. If they are tests of the same achievement they must be composed of items meeting the same task specifications and hence drawn from the same item pool. Yet if one set is biased and the other is unbiased, there must be some systematic difference between them. To show bias we must show the tests to be the same and yet to be different. This is obviously a logical impossibility. For this reason demonstration of bias in a properly validated achievement test is impossible, and if bias cannot be demonstrated, there is no good reason to believe that it exists (Ebel, 1977:39).

On the other hand, if bias *does* exist, perhaps Ebel has not tried hard enough to find methods of demonstrating it, and perhaps some of the standard approaches to the analysis of tests are inadequate for this task.

Let us examine items from widely used tests of reading comprehension: the Stanford Diagnostic Reading Test, the Canadian Test of Basic Skills (a revision of the Iowa Test of Basic Skills for Canadian use), the Gates McGinitie Reading Test, the Nelson-Denny Reading Test and the Gapadol Reading Comprehension Test. These items have been chosen to show a range of cultural knowledge and have been altered for reasons of brevity. In each case the form of the test and the item number is given so that the original can be identified.

In these test items a student will have to rely on specific sociocultural knowledge to get the right answer. In turn, cultural knowledge covers various aspects of a specific human society, including its history, geography (e.g., animals, plants, climate), literature, art, social institutions (e.g., law, government), family life, housing, nutrition, customs, cultural attitudes and values.

1. *Patriotic objects:* There are red and white stripes and white stars in our flag. Our flag contains one_____ for every state.

   (a) stripe   (b) star   (S.D.R.T. Form X. Level 1. #3)

2. *Food:* In the story the French regarded potatoes like most Canadians regard:

   (a) spinach   (b) tomatoes   (c) horsemeat   (d) margarine
                                                         (C.T.B.S. Form 1. #89)

(Note: in the story, the French dislike potatoes.)

3. *Customs:* In this poem, what does April Fool! mean?

   (a) The person who said it was fooling.

   (b) It was not April at all.   (C.C.T.B.S. Form 1. #98)

4. *Games:* Sam won at marbles because he could_____ straighter than Bill.

   (a) show   (b) shoot   (c) draw   (d) run
                                                         (G. McG.D. Form 3M. #1)

5. *History:* In the first colonies in America, making clothing took time. The women first had to spin the yarn. Clothes for the colonial family were usually made in _____ .

    (a) factories   (b) homes   (c) luxury   (d) China

    (G. McG.D. Form 3M. #14)

6. *Geography:* The Yankee peddler traded as far west as the Mississippi and as far south as Louisiana. He operated _____ .

    (a) over most of the country

    (b) as far south as Louisiana

    (N.D. Form D. #10)

7. *Folklore:* Pam went to the party with a tall pointed hat, long black cape and a broom. She was dressed as a _____ .

    (a) witch   (b) ghost   (c) cowgirl   (d) pumpkin

    (G. McG.C. Form 1. #4)

8. *Housing:* Bill ran out on his front porch to watch the firetruck. He lives in

    _____ .

    (a) a big apartment   (b) a city house   (c) a trailer

    (C.T.B.S. Form 4. Level 9. #1)

9. *Culture-bound metaphors:* What does applying soft soap mean in paragraph 6?

    (a) looking clean in public

    (b) flattering people

    (C.T.B.S. Form 1. #131)

10. *Stories familiar to particular cultural groups:* (Cloze text example)
    The person was holding tight to the handle of an open _____ , dangling by one hand like a doll tied to the string of a balloon . . . .

    (Note: the answer is 'umbrella')

Test items 1–10 require a knowledge of (successively): the symbolism of the United States flag; Canadian food preferences; April first customs; how the game of marbles is played; early American history; American geography; the garb of the typical witch; the layout of different types of North American homes; an English idiom; and the story of Mary Poppins. It is clear that special cultural knowledge is required. Therefore, contrary to Ebel's claim, cultural bias does exist in reading comprehension texts.

Though cultural bias clearly exists, is the presence of bias an important matter? Certainly at least three of the tests from which items (1–10) are drawn are widely used: the Stanford Diagnostic Reading Test, the Gates-McGinitie and the Canadian Test of Basic Skills. Moreover, the frequency and distribution of biased items in these widely used tests is important. The percentage of biased items in a test can be counted. My investigation (Mohan, 1979) of the Canadian Test of Basic Skills, Form 1 (grades 3–8) indicates that 7% of the items are biased. This is by no means negligible in its likely effect on the scores of culturally different students. Moreover the biased items are unevenly distributed, so that in the fifth grade section of the test the percentage of biased items is 15%. Other tests show such clustering too. Thus the Gates-McGinitie Primary C Form 1 test contains 10% biased items, and in the Stanford Diagnostic Reading Test Form X Level 1, the percentage rises to 16%. These percentages are high enough to have a marked effect on scores. In addition, these figures are somewhat conservative and almost certainly understimate the amount of bias. Items which are borderline cases have not been counted. And as a member of the host culture, I am likely to overlook some of the less obvious cases of bias.

The decisions that can be made about individual students on the basis of biased reading comprehension tests are not trivial. Reading comprehension scores are often used to assign students to reading groups of different levels of competence. Here a biased result is likely to lead to incorrect diagnosis of difficulties in reading and inappropriate teaching. More serious is the situation in some schools where reading comprehension scores are the means for placing students in streams of different general academic ability, i.e., a low score puts students in a slow class, possibly for the rest of their school career. When a reading comprehension score is used as an index of academic ability, a biased score and the decision following from it can have all the force of a self-fulfilling prophecy.

Even if it is accepted that bias exists in quantity and that it may affect important decisions, some might argue that bias is not a matter worthy of serious attention. One argument is that students should be tested on cultural knowledge, since they will not be able to function properly in North American society if they do not learn about North American culture. Although it is certainly appropriate to test for cultural knowledge, such testing should not be confounded with reading comprehension. Cultural knowledge should be tested separately, specifically, and systematically, as some modern language teachers do.

Some teachers do not believe that cultural knowledge should be tested separately. They assert that special cultural knowledge should be a necessary part of reading comprehension tests. This argument has been advanced by competent and thoughtful ESL teachers, and is based on the claims that special cultural knowledge will inevitably occur in reading materials that students will have to deal with, and that a reading test should faithfully reflect the reading tasks and materials facing the student.

While there are a number of objections to be made here (e.g., how much special cultural knowledge is actually required by a math textbook?), the crux of the problem is that this view concentrates on the students' performance but ignores the evaluation being made of that performance. Suppose two students give the wrong answer to a reading comprehension item. One student is native born, the other is a recent immigrant. The former may be weak in reading comprehension, the latter may be missing some cultural knowledge. The task they both face is the same, but the interpretation of what they do should be different. The immigrant is not necessarily weak in reading comprehension despite the incorrect answer choice. Where evaluation is incorrect, remediation will also be incorrect.

How can the consumers of tests identify bias?

One procedure that can be used to identify biased items is to ask the following two questions:

Question A
Does the item test only language knowledge or does it test knowledge of the world too?

Question B
Does the item test:

a) knowledge of the world which is available to all cultures, or

b) knowledge of the world which is readily available only to particular cultural groups

It might seem that knowledge of the world concerning witches and Halloween is needed to answer the following item:

11. The playmates wore costumes to Sandra's Halloween party. Nellie_____ a tall, black, pointed hat.

    (a) walked   (b) wore   (c) cared   (d) hurt   (e) looked

    (G. McG. D. Form 3M. #7)

Yet on closer inspection, it becomes clear that the item can be answered on the basis of language knowledge since *wore* (answer b) is the only one which fills the slot to make a semantically acceptable sentence. It is ungrammatical to say that she walked, cared, or looked a hat and it is nonsensical to say that she hurt one.

12. Sam and Bill played the whole day. In the evening they felt_____.

    (a) rested   (b) small   (c) tired

    (S.D.R.T. Form X. Level 1. #17)

Item (12) tests knowledge of the world. This, not language knowledge, is the basis for seeing a connection between playing all day and feeling tired. However, since it is reasonable to assume that every cultural group would see such a connection, the item does not depend on a piece of special cultural information. It does not test knowledge of the world available only to particular cultural groups.

    Thus by asking our two key questions (Questions A and B) we can see that items (11) and (12) are not considered to be culturally biased, although at first they might have appeared to be. On the other hand, items (1–10 on page 124–125) are considered culturally biased, for in each case special cultural information is required, and that information is readily available only to particular cultural groups.

How can teachers identify bias and what actions can they take? They can investigate the items in the reading comprehension test currently used in their school and in any other available reading test which might be used in its place. The procedure for doing so has been outlined above. Group discussion of the items, either with other teachers or with ESL students, works well. The lone reader often passes over difficulties that a group will detect and may also make cultural assumptions that ESL students would not. Further, the procedure is justifiable as a learning activity, since it requires careful reading and interpretation. If the current reading comprehension test turns out to be more biased than an available alternative, then a case can be made for switching to the alternative test. Secondly, once biased items have been noted, teachers can check to see that the bias is taken into account in the interpretation of test scores and in the decisions about students based on the interpretation.

Is cultural bias in reading comprehension tests inevitable?

What has been demonstrated so far is that some test items confound language knowledge and cultural experience. In effect these items are not simply testing the ability to read the comprehension passage, they are testing for other information as well. As such, they are poor tests of reading comprehension. The maker of standardized tests has certain procedures of statistical item-analysis which are intended to ensure that items meet standards of validity and reliability, yet these do not seem to have been successful in eliminating culturally biased items in the tests examined. One reason for this is that the initial scrutiny of items for suitability (or content validity) is very crude and allows the biased items in. This content validity check needs to be refined. The remedy offered here (See Questions A and B.) is to relate the analysis of items to semantic theory in order to show that such analysis can be based on semantic principles. This is helpful for clarifying both cultural bias and the general validity of reading comprehension items.

6.3 COMPREHENSION AND SEMANTIC THEORY

An important part of competence in reading comprehension is the ability to draw inferences from written text. Research in reading must therefore investigate the nature of inference. Semantic theory is centrally concerned with the nature of inference (or implication or consequence) in language; it offers a principled basis for saying whether one sentence can be inferred from another. If the role of inference in reading comprehension test items is made clear, the connection between the analysis of these items and semantic theory can be shown.

The following item is a clear example of the inference/implication/consequence relation:

13. . . . . Three girls put frosting on the cakes that had cooled. We learned a new word for frosting. At the bakery it was called icing . . . .

Q: What were the three girls doing?

A: (i) cooling the cakes

  (ii) putting icing on the cakes

  (iii) making frosting for the cakes

(C.T.B.S. Form 1. #9)

Is it possible to infer the right answer (ii) from the passage? The passage implies that answer ii is 'true', for it asks the reader to decide whether *three girls put frosting on the cakes that had cooled* implies *the girls were putting icing on the cakes*, where *icing* can be substituted for *frosting*. One way to check the appropriateness of this implication is whether *therefore* or *consequently* can be inserted between these two sentences but not between the passage sentence and the other possible answers. And the passage gives no grounds for choosing the other answers. It does not imply answer (i) and it does not imply answer (iii). They are unknown. The general form of the relations between the passage and possible answers is given below.

- The passage implies the right answer sentence (the sentence is true).

- The passage doesn't imply the wrong answer sentence (the sentence is unknown).

- The passage contradicts the wrong answer sentence (the sentence is false).

This can be simplified further to whether one sentence (S1) implies another sentence (S2) below:

- S1 implies S2. True? False? Unknown?

This is the typical pattern for reading comprehension test items: the correct answer sentence can be inferred from one passage sentence (or a combination of passage sentences), and more generally, the student is being asked to judge whether one sentence follows from another or not. In this way inference plays a central role in reading comprehension items.

There are a number of variant forms of the pattern S1 implies S2. For example, the item about Sam and Bill playing the whole day (12) takes a different form, in that most of the answer sentence is part of the passage. Yet when the correct word is inserted, the second sentence follows from the first. *Sam and Bill played the whole day* implies *In the evening they felt tired*. It does not imply the possible sentence made by the insertions of *rested* or *small*. It thus conforms to the general form of S1 implies S2. However, this is not to say that every comprehension question conforms to this pattern. Cloze items like (10) minimally require that the word inserted in the slot should complete the sentence to form a semantically acceptable sentence. If that is all that is required in an item, then it is demanding recognition of relations within a sentence. The item is not demanding recognition of inference, which is a relation between sentences.

The concept of inference has an important bearing on the analysis of cultural bias. It has already been noted that the cultural bias problem in reading comprehension tests arises because both language knowledge and cultural knowledge are required in these tests. Clearly it would be helpful to distinguish between language knowledge and cultural knowledge in a principled way. The question about icing and frosting (13) tests language knowledge, and the one about how witches dress (7) tests cultural knowledge. Both require the recognition of an inference. The inference in the former is based on language knowledge and the inference in the latter is based on cultural knowledge. The distinction between these two kinds of inference is almost identical to the distinction semanticists like Katz and Leech have made between semantic and factual inference. Semantic inference is based on knowledge of language, and factual inference is based on knowledge of the world (including cultural knowledge).

6.4 SEMANTIC INFERENCE AND FACTUAL INFERENCE

Linguistic semantics distinguishes carefully between the relation of (14a) to (14b) and the relation of (15a) to (15b):

14. a. He is a bachelor.

    b. He is an unmarried man.

15. a. He is Pierre Trudeau.

    b. He is a former Canadian Prime Minister.

(14) is a case of semantic inference. We know that (b) follows from (a) because of our knowledge of the English language. If we were challenged to prove it, we could draw on linguistic analysis and the grammar and dictionary of English. It is this kind of knowledge that is central in tests of language knowledge and skill. (15) is a case of factual inference. We know that (b) follows from (a) because of our knowledge of the world. To prove it we would go to yearbooks of Canadian facts and ultimately to the encyclopedia. This is the kind of knowledge that is central in achievement tests.

Linguistic semanticists are interested in semantic inference as contrasted with factual inference because a main job of linguistic semantics is to describe and explain inference in language. We can look at semantic analyses of verb tenses, prepositions, articles, and the structure of vocabulary, for instance, as ways of accounting for the semantic inference relations between sentences. To account for all the semantic inference relations in English is an enormous task, only a fragment of which has been completed, and its application to examples from everyday discourse is difficult. Nevertheless, the analysis of semantic inference offers a systematic method of procedure, secured by a well-argued basis in language theory.

Some linguists have been interested in testing native speaker judgments of semantic inference and have constructed semantic test items in written form to do so. These test items show parallels with reading comprehension items. Both kinds of items require knowledge of semantic inference. Both get the individual to read and interpret the test item (the 'passage' and the 'answers'). However, the semantic test item is different in that it has a different purpose: to find out more about semantic theory. And it is aimed narrowly at a single specific case of a semantic inference relation.

By contrast, when we look at actual items from reading comprehension tests, we generally find that a long and complex chain of inference occurs. What we need to do is check to see if steps of factual inference occur in the chain, and then we need to consider whether the factual knowledge is culturally bound. This, in fact, is what was suggested in Questions A and B on page 127. In other words we satisfy ourselves that the student does not need special cultural knowledge to arrive at the answer. We use our linguistic intuitions to make this judgment. Linguistic semantics sharpens our sense of the relevant distinctions, provides principled grounds for making such judgments, and helps us to make out justifications according to public criteria.

Even though it is not uncontroversial and not without borderline problems, the distinction between semantic inference and factual inference is based on clearly argued principles (Katz, 1972, p.117ff; Leech, 1974, p.7ff), and the same arguments can be used to establish the distinction between language knowledge and cultural knowledge in test items. In addition, a major achievement of linguistic semantics is the detailed analysis of semantic inference in natural language. This means that the analysis of semantic inference in reading comprehension test items can be supported by a developed body of knowledge. This is not to say that the body of knowledge is complete and the analysis is automatic, for a great deal still needs to be done. Yet it is clear that the analysis can be systematic.

6.5 INFERENCE IN TESTING

Figure 6.1 shows different types of tests and different bases for inference. All of these tests require the student to read, but they differ in their aims.

Reading comprehension tests aim to test knowledge of language through reading.

Figure 6.1

Bases for Inference in Tests

Test Type	Aim of Test	Main Type of Inference	Additional Requirement	Bias Against Second Language Learner
A. Reading comprehension tests	knowledge of language	semantic inference	general knowledge of the world	cultural knowledge assumed
B. Achievement tests	knowledge of a subject area	factual inference	reading comprehension	high reading level assumed
C. Culture tests	knowledge of a culture	factual inference	reading comprehension	high reading level assumed

They require semantic inference. They also assume general commonsense knowledge of the world. When they assume special cultural knowledge, they are biased against second language learners. *Achievement tests* aim to test knowledge of a subject area and require factual inference. They also assume reading comprehension. If they assume a high level of reading comprehension they are biased against second language learners. *Culture tests* aim at knowledge of the culture and require factual inference.

The basis for semantic inference is knowledge of the language. By contrast, the basis for factual inference is knowledge of the world. Knowledge of the world can be divided into general common sense knowledge of the world, knowledge of culture and special area subject knowledge.

Above we discussed reading comprehension tests (A in Figure 6.1). We now turn to tests of content (B and C in Figure 6.1). These call for factual inference.

One type of content test is a test of cultural knowledge. H.N. Seelye describes "cultural assimilators," which are items designed to test specifically for cultural knowledge:

16. As a young American tourist in Tours, France, you have been invited to dinner at the home of a French business associate of your father. You know that under such circumstances it is considered polite to bring a bouquet of flowers to the hostess. Accordingly, you arrive at the door of the apartment with a handsome bouquet of white chrysanthemums. As your hostess greets you, you offer the bouquet to her. You notice a look of surprise and distaste cross her countenance before she masters herself and accepts your offering graciously.

   All evening you are haunted by the feeling that you have done something wrong. You would like to apologize—but you are at a loss to know what for. What could explain your hostess's reaction?

   (i) A bouquet of chrysanthemums is considered an apology for a serious blunder in French culture.

   (ii) A bouquet of chrysanthemums is considered a proposal of marriage in French culture.

   (iii) Chrysanthemums are considered the flower of death in French culture.

   (iv) The hostess was allergic to chrysanthemums.   (Seelye, 1974:108).

The correct answer is (iii). Armed with this item of French cultural knowledge, we can draw the factual inference that a French hostess presented with such a bouquet would be unpleasantly surprised. Such direct tests of cultural knowledge can play a valuable role in second language education.

Of course content tests testing cultural knowledge are unusual. The most frequent type of test of content knowledge is in the achievement test (B in Figure 6.1), where specialized knowledge of a subject area is at issue as in tests of biology, chemistry, geography, economics, psychology, and so on. The following geography example is typical of the kind of item which appears in examinations for prospective graduate students.

17. The fact that Tacoma, Washington, has a growing season of 245 days, while Atlanta, Georgia, has a growing season of 224 days can best be explained by the

(i) latitude of Tacoma as compared with the latitude of Atlanta.

(ii) longitude of Tacoma as compared with the longitude of Atlanta.

(iii) marine climate of Tacoma.

(iv) humid subtropical climate of Atlanta.

To get the right answer (iii), a complicated sequence of factual reasoning is needed, taking into account both the geographical position of Atlanta and Tacoma and the influence of different climatic types on the growing season, as well as rejecting the distracting information about longitude and latitude. All of this calls for specialized geographic knowledge, which is quite legitimate, for the item is aimed at discriminating between those students who have an adequate knowledge of geography and an ability to reason geographically, and those students who do not.

The difference between a reading comprehension item and an achievement test item as in this geography example, like the difference between knowledge of language and knowledge of the world, is so obvious that it hardly seems to merit discussion. Yet even here problems arise when language knowledge and content knowledge are intertwined, as they often are. The geography question assumes that the test-taker can manage a certain level of reading comprehension successfully, because the student has to read the item and understand that what is demanded is not an explanation of the growing season in Atlanta, but an explanation of the longer growing season in Tacoma. Many achievement tests assume a threshold level of reading comprehension. A second language learner who is a capable mathematician may perform poorly on word problems in mathematics tests because of the language barrier. In cases like these it becomes clear how knowledge of language is a necessary condition for demonstrating content knowledge.

Reading comprehension tests can be biased if the content factor looms too large: that is, if they demand special cultural knowledge or if they require special subject knowledge. This is where analysis is needed of the intertwining of language and content. In tests of language knowledge and use, items often assume knowledge of content information. If an individual lacks this content knowledge, the item becomes a test of content knowledge, not of language knowledge. If standard procedures of test analysis cannot detect this, then linguistic analysis is needed.

A comparable problem can arise with achievement tests if they demand too high a level of reading comprehension of the student. Just as there is a problem with language tests when the content factor is too high, so there is a problem with content tests when the language factor is too high.

6.6 SUMMARY
AND CONCLUSION

Items like (1–10) are not appropriate reading comprehension questions for ESL students because they require special cultural knowledge which is available only to particular cultural groups. Such special knowledge should not be incorporated into reading tests. Reading tests should essentially test the ability to use knowledge of the language and reading skills to get meaning from the printed page. It is the task of achievement tests (of biology, social studies, and so on) to test for nonlinguistic knowledge. It is legitimate to draw on nonlinguistic knowledge in a reading comprehension test only where it plays a neutral, supporting role, and is common to all students properly assigned to take the test. It should be standard policy to eliminate specific cultural items from tests when those taking the test include culturally different groups. In fact, eliminating material irrelevant to the aims of the test would be likely to improve the test for all groups. If the item tests knowledge of the world available only to particular cultural groups, it should be discarded. Linguistic semantic theory plays a crucial role in establishing the major distinctions required and in providing the detailed semantic description necessary to put the procedure on a systematic basis.

Greater awareness is needed of the content factor in language tests and of the language factor in content tests. If either of these is too high, it will cause problems. Problems are particularly likely to occur when tests developed for students of one language and culture are taken by students of a different language and a different culture.

The intertwining of language and content can be a positive advantage in many aspects of education. But in testing and evaluation it is a source of disadvantage for the second language learner.

To reduce this disadvantage, we need to distinguish between semantic inference and factual inference. Here the language teacher has an important role to play as an advocate for the students' best interests.

EXERCISES FOR
CHAPTER SIX

1. Choose a short piece of literature in English (or another second language) that assumes some background of cultural understanding e.g., a poem, a short story, an essay. Read it with a group of second language learners. Discuss their interpretation of it. What do they find difficult to understand? How is their interpretation different from yours? List some of the items of cultural knowledge which influence their interpretation.

2. Pick a reading comprehension test that might be used on your students. Apply the procedure outlined in Questions A and B on page 127 in the chapter. Identify any items which seem to be culturally biased.

3. Try out some multiple-choice reading comprehension items with a group of second language learners. Ask students to pick the answer they feel is right. Then discuss with them why they feel that answer is right and why they rejected the alternative answers.

4. Design a culture assimilator. An example is given in item (16) in the chapter. Seelye, *Teaching Culture*, gives more examples and discusses them. Assimilators contain:

   a) a short passage demonstrating an intercultural exchange in which a misunderstanding occurs.

b) four possible interpretations of what transpired.

c) feedback to the reader as to the correct answer.

5. Find an achievement test that is appropriate for your students in level and content. Pick a student who is knowledgeable in the content area. Try out parts of the test with the student, asking the student to explain the reasoning behind the answer he chooses. Do you find that any of the items are answered incorrectly because of reading problems?

6. Make your own 'test of tests'. Gunnarson, in *Language in Education: Testing the Tests*, made up a 'test of tests.' Ten items were selected from widely used intelligence, personality, and achievement tests. The reader of the test was asked to judge whether an item comes from an intelligence, personality, achievement, or language test—or "none of the above." The judgment can be difficult to make, and suggests that many of these tests may be measuring language proficiency to a large extent. See also Oller, *Language Tests at School*.

7. Read articles which are critical of claims that tests are biased. What would count as good evidence of test bias? A useful source is C.R. Reynolds, 1982, "The problem of Bias in Psychological Assessment," in C.R. Reynolds and T.B. Gutkin (eds.), *The Handbook of School Psychology*, pp. 178–208, New York: John Wiley.

CHAPTER SIX
SUGGESTED READINGS

Anastasi, A. 1976. *Psychological Testing*. (3rd ed.). New York: Collier-Macmillan. Contains a discussion of the use of culture-fair tests.

Condon, J. and F. Yousef. 1975. *An Introduction to Intercultural Communication*. Indianapolis, Indiana: Bobbs-Merrill. Reviews a variety of issues in intercultural communication.

Flaughter, R. 1978. "The Many Definitions of Test Bias." *American Psychologist 33*, 7:671–679. A discussion of the ways in which tests might be biased.

Gunnarson, B. 1978. "A Look at Content Similarities Between Intelligence, Achievement, Personality and Language Tests." In J. Oller and K. Perkins. *Language Education: Testing the Tests*. Rowley, Mass.: Newbury House. Looks at the similarities in various different types of standardized educational tests by taking a close look at test items and seeing what they require the examinees to do.

Mohan, B.A. 1979. "Cultural Bias in Reading Comprehension Tests." *On TESOL 79*:171–177. This publication, *On TESOL '79*, also contains a number of other articles on bias in testing.

Oller, J. 1979. *Language Tests at School*. London: Longman. An overview of language testing which looks at the over-lap between the constructs of language proficiency, intelligence, and academic ability.

Pearn, M. 1978. *Employment Testing and the Goal of Equal Opportunity: the American Experience*. London: The Runnymede Trust. Reviews American work on the question of test bias and discrimination in employment selection and relates it to the British context. An aspect of the Runnymede Trust's work on the collection and dissemination of information and the promotion of public education on immigration and race relations.

Seelye, H. 1974. *Teaching Culture: Strategies for Foreign Language Educators*. Skokie, Ill.: National Textbook Co. A practical guide, with useful activities for classroom discussion, which offers specific insights into how cultures may differ.

References

References

Allen, J., and J. Howard. 1981. "Subject-Related ESL: An Experiment in Communicative Language Teaching." *Canadian Modern Language Review* 37:535–550.

Allen, J., and H. Widdowson. 1974. *English in Physical Science*. Oxford: Oxford University Press.

American Association for the Advancement of Science. 1970. *Science: A Process Approach*. Waltham, Mass.: Xerox.

Anastasi, A. 1976. *Psychological Testing* (3d ed.). New York: Collier-Macmillan.

Arnott. M. (unpublished) "Adapting a Social Studies Unit for ESL Students." Term paper for Education 508, University of British Columbia.

Asher, J. 1977. *Learning Another Language Through Actions: The Complete Teacher's Guidebook*. Los Gatos: Sky Oaks Productions.

Ashworth, M. 1975. *Immigrant Children and Canadian Schools*. Toronto: McLelland and Stewart.

Bander, R. 1971. *American English Rhetoric*. New York: Holt, Rinehart and Winston.

Barndt, D., F. Cristall, and D. Marino. 1982. *Getting There: Producing Photostories with Immigrant Women*. Toronto: Between the Lines.

Barnes, D. 1976. *From Communication to Curriculum*. Harmondsworth, Middlesex: Penguin Books.

Bates, M., and T. Dudley-Evans. 1976. *Nucleus General Science*. London: Longman.

Billows, F. 1961. *The Techniques of Language Teaching*. London: Longman.

Blosser, B. 1979. *English for Adult Living*. Silver Springs, Md: Institute of Modern Languages.

Brown, D. 1979. *Mother Tongue to English: The Young Child in the Multicultural School*. Cambridge: Cambridge University Press.

Brubacher, J. 1947. *A History of the Problems of Education*. New York: McGraw Hill.

Bruner, J. 1960. *The Process of Education*. Cambridge, Mass.: Harvard University Press.

Bruner, J., et al. 1970. *Man: A Course of Study*. Washington D.C.: Curriculum Development Associates.

Bruner, J. 1975. "Language as an Instrument of Thought." In A. Davies (ed.). *Problems of Language and Learning*. London: Heinemann.

Bullock Committee. 1975. *A Language for Life*. London: HMSO.

Candlin C. and C. Edelhoff. 1982. *Challenges: Teacher's Guide*. London: Longman.

Cantieni, G., and R. Tremblay. 1973. "The Use of Concrete Mathematical Situations in Learning a Second Language." *TESOL Quarterly* 7(3):165–174.

Catterson, J. 1965. "Successful Study Skills Programs." In H. Herber (ed.) *Developing Study Skills in Secondary Schools*. Newark, Delaware: International Reading Association, pp. 156–169.

Cazden, C. B. 1972. *Child Language and Education*. New York: Holt, Rinehart and Winston.

Cazden, C. B. 1977. "Language, Literacy and Literature." *The National Elementary Principal* 57(1):40–52.

Chamot, A. 1983. "Toward a Functional ESL Curriculum in the Elementary School." *TESOL Quarterly* 17(3):459–471.

Chappell, M., L. Coulter, J. Kidder, and A. Shorthouse. 1981. *Centennial Museum ESL Resource Book*. Vancouver, B. C. Vancouver School Board.

Cohen, A., and M. Swain. 1976. "Bilingual Education: The Immersion Model." *TESOL Quarterly* 10(1):45–54.

Condon, J., and F. Yousef. 1975. *An Introduction to Intercultural Communication*. Indianapolis, Indiana: Bobbs–Merrill.

Cooper, J. 1979. *Think and Link*. London: Edward Arnold.

Corder, S. P. 1966. *The Visual Element in Language Teaching*. London: Longman.

Corder, S. P. 1973. *Introducing Applied Linguistics*. Harmondsworth, Middlesex: Penguin Books.

Cummins, J. 1979. "Linguistic Interdependence and the Educational Development of Bilingual Children." *Review of Educational Research* 49(2):222–251.

Cummins, J. 1981. "Age on Arrival and Immigrant Second Language Learning in Canada: A Reassessment." *Applied Linguistics* 2:132–149.

Cummins, J. 1981. *Bilingualism and Minority-Language Children*. Toronto: Ontario Institute for Studies in Education.

Cummins, J. 1983. "Language Proficiency and Academic Achievement." In J. Oller (ed.). 1983. *Issues in Language Testing Research*. Rowley, Mass.: Newbury House.

Dale, E. 1954. *Audio-Visual Methods in Teaching* (rev. ed.). New York: Holt, Rinehart and Winston.

D'Anglejan, A. 1978. "Language Learning in and out of Classrooms." In J. Richards (ed.) *Understanding Second and Foreign Language Learning*, 218–237. Rowley, Mass.: Newbury House.

Danto, A. C. 1975. *Sartre*. Glasgow: Fontana/Collins.

Davies, E., and S. Hadi. 1973. *Scope, Book Three: Ready for Work*. London: Longman.

Dearden, R. F. 1968. *The Philosophy of Primary Education*. London: Routledge and Kegan Paul.

Dewey, J. 1900. *The Child and the Curriculum; The School and Society*. Chicago: The University of Chicago Press.

Dewey, J. 1916. *Democracy and Education*. New York: Macmillan.

Dewey, J. 1938. *Experience and Education*. New York: Macmillan.

Dulay, H., K. Burt, and S. Krashen. 1982. *Language Two*. New York: Oxford University Press.

Dworkin, M. 1959. *Dewey on Education*. New York: Columbia University Press.

Earle, R. A. 1976. *Teaching Reading and Mathematics*. Newark, Delaware: International Reading Association.

Early, M., C. Thew, and P. Wakefield. Forthcoming, 1985. *ESL Instruction via the Regular Curriculum: A Framework and Resource Book*. Victoria, B.C.: Ministry of Education, British Columbia.

Ebel, R. L. 1977. *The Uses of Standardized Testing*. Bloomington, Indiana: The Phi Delta Kappa Foundation.

English Language Services. 1966. *Special English: Medicine, Book I*. New York: Collier-Macmillan International.

Faerch, C., and G. Kasper (eds.). 1982. *Strategies in Interlanguage Communication*. London: Longman.

Fillmore, L. W. 1982. "The Language Learner as an Individual." *On TESOL '82*. Washington, D.C.: TESOL.

Finocchiaro, M., and M. Bonomo. 1973. *The Foreign Language Learner: A Guide for Teachers*. New York: Regents.

Flaugher, R. 1978. "The Many Definitions of Test Bias." *American Psychologist* 33(7):671–679.

Frankena, W. 1965. *Three Historical Philosophies of Education*. Chicago: Scott, Foresman.

Garvie, E. 1976. *Breakthrough to Fluency*. Oxford: Blackwell.

Gerbrandt, G. 1974. *An Idea Book for Acting Out and Writing Language K-8*. Urbana, Ill.: National Council of Teachers of English.

Giere, R. 1979. *Understanding Scientific Reasoning*. New York: Holt, Rinehart and Winston.

Glendinning, E. 1974. *English in Mechanical Engineering*. London: Oxford University Press.

Goffman, E. 1974. *Frame Analysis*. New York: Harper and Row.

Gosch, M., and R. Hammer. 1974. *The Last Testament of Lucky Luciano*. New York: Dell Publishing.

Gubbay, D. 1978. *The Use of Role Playing in Communication Training*. Southall, Middlesex: National Center for Industrial Language Training.

Gunnarson, B. 1978. "A Look at Content Similarities Between Intelligence, Achievement, Personality and Language Tests." In J. Oller and K. Perkins. *Language Education: Testing the Tests*. Rowley, Mass.: Newbury House.

Halliday, M. A. K., and R. Hasan. 1976. *Cohesion in English*. London: Longman.

Hanna, P., C. Kohn, J. Lee, and C. Ver Steeg. 1970 *Investigating Man's World, Metropolitan Studies, Teacher's Edition*. Glenview, Illinois: Scott, Foresman.

Harvey, D. 1969. *Explanation in Geography*. New York: St. Martin's Press.

Herber, H. (ed.). 1965. *Developing Study Skills in Secondary Schools*. Newark, Delaware: International Reading Association.

Herber, H. 1970. *Teaching Reading in the Content Areas*. Englewood Cliffs, N.J.: Prentice-Hall.

Herber, H. 1978. *Teaching Reading in the Content Areas* (2d ed.). Englewood Cliffs, N.J.: Prentice-Hall.

Howe, L., and M. Howe. 1975. *Personalizing Education: Values Clarification and Beyond*. New York: Hart Publishing Co.

Joyce, J. 1916. *A Portrait of the Artist as a Young Man*. Harmondsworth, Middlesex: Penguin Books.

Jupp, T., and S. Hodlin. 1975. *Industrial English*. London: Heinemann.

Katz, J. J. 1972. *Semantic Theory*. New York: Harper and Row.

Kerlinger, F. 1973. *Foundations of Behavioural Research* (2d ed.). New York: Holt, Rinehart and Winston.

Kernan, D. 1974. *Steps to English, Book I, Teacher's Edition*. New York: McGraw-Hill.

Kettering, J. 1975. *Developing Communicative Competence: Interaction Activities in English as a Second Language*. Pittsburgh: The University Center for International Studies.

Krashen, S. 1982. *Principles and Practice in Second Language Acquisition*. Oxford: Pergamon.

Laird, E. 1977. *Introduction to Functional Language Training in the Work Place*. Southall, Middlesex: National Centre for Industrial Language Training.

Landa, L. N. 1974. *Algorithmization in Learning and Instruction*. Englewood Cliffs, N.J.: Educational Technology Publishers.

Lawrence, M. 1972. *Writing as a Thinking Process*. Ann Arbor: University of Michigan Press.

Lawrence, M. 1975. *Reading, Thinking, Writing*. Ann Arbor: University of Michigan Press.

Leech, G. 1974. *Semantics*. Harmondsworth, Middlesex: Penguin Books.

Leech, G., and J. Svartvik. 1975. *A Communicative Grammar of English*. London: Longman.

LeGallais, E., et al. 1981. *ESL Through Food Skills*. Vancouver, B.C.: Vancouver School Board.

Letkeman, P. 1973. *Crime as Work*. Englewood Cliffs, N.J.: Prentice-Hall.

Levine, J. 1970. *Scope, Stage 2: Teacher's Book*. London: Longman.

Levine, J., H. Hester, and G. Skirrow. 1972. *Scope, Stage 2*. London: Longman.

Levinson, S. 1983. *Pragmatics*. Cambridge: Cambridge University Press.

Lewis, B. N., I. Horabin, and C. Gare. 1967. *Flowcharts, Logical Trees and Algorithms for Rules and Regulations: CAS Occasional Paper No. 2*. London: HMSO.

Long, M. 1983. "Does Second Language Instruction Make a Difference? A Review of Research." *TESOL Quarterly* 17(3):359–382.

Lynskey, A. 1974. *Children and Themes*. Oxford: Oxford University Press.

MacFarlane, T. 1979. *Literacy in Action*. London: Macmillan.

Mackay, R., and A. Mountford (eds.). 1978. *English for Specific Purposes*. London: Longman.

Mackey, W. 1965. *Language Teaching Analysis*. London: Longman.

Maley, A., and A. Duff. 1978. *Drama Techniques in Language Learning*. Cambridge: Cambridge University Press.

Margolis, S. 1971. *Special English: The Department Store*. London: Collier-Macmillan.

Marland, M. 1977. *Language Across the Curriculum*. London: Heinemann.

Martin, N., et al. 1976. *Writing and Learning Across the Curriculum 11–16*. London: Ward Lock.

Martinez, F. 1984. *Elementary ESL in the Content Areas*. (Unpublished paper presented to the TESOL 1984 Convention, Houston, Texas.)

Mason, C. 1971. "The Relevance of Intensive Training in English as a Foreign Language for University Students." *Language Learning* 21(2):197–204.

McCready, G. 1972. "Developing a Lesson Around a Dialogue." In K. Croft (ed.) *Readings on English as a Second Language*, 106–114. Cambridge, Mass.: Winthrop.

McKim, R. 1980. *Experiences in Visual Thinking* (2d ed.). Monterey, California: Brooks/Cole.

McNeil, J. 1981. *Curriculum: A Comprehensive Introduction*. (2d ed.). Boston: Little, Brown and Company.

Meredith, P. 1961. *Learning, Remembering and Knowing*. London: The English Universities Press.

Merritt, J., et al. 1977. *Developing Independence in Reading*. Milton Keynes: The Open University Press.

Moffett, J. 1968(a). *A Student-Centered Language Arts Curriculum, Grades K-13*. Boston: Houghton Mifflin.

Moffett, J. 1968. *Teaching the Universe of Discourse*. Boston: Houghton Mifflin.

Moffett, J., and B. Wagner. 1976. *Student-Centered Language Arts and Reading K-13*. Boston: Houghton Mifflin.

Mohan, B. A. 1973. "Comprehension as Semantics Plus Induction." *Linguistics* 115:93–105.

Mohan, B. A. 1974(a). "Principles, Postulates and Politeness." *Chicago Linguistic Society Papers* 10:446–459.

Mohan, B. A. 1974(b). "Do Sequencing Rules Exist?" *Semiotica* 12(1):75–96.

Mohan B. A. 1975. "Sociolinguistics and Context-Dependence." In P. Luelsdorf (ed.) *Linguistic Perspectives on Black English*, 91–106. Nürnberg: Verlag Hans Carl.

Mohan, B. A. 1976. "Discourse, Context and Languages for Specialised Purposes." In L. Trimble (ed) *Languages for Specialised Purposes*. Stuttgart: Fourth International Congress of Applied Linguistics.

Mohan, B. A. 1977(a). "Situations and English for Specialized Purposes." *English for Specialized Purposes Newsletter*, 3. Corvallis: Oregon State University.

Mohan, B. A. 1977(b). "Towards a Situational Curriculum." *On TESOL* 1977:250–257. Washington, D.C.: TESOL.

Mohan, B. A. 1979(a). "Tests as Interethnic Communication." *Proceedings of the Canadian Ethnology Society*.

Mohan, B. A. 1979(b). "Cultural Bias in Reading Comprehension Tests." *On TESOL '79*:171–177. Washington, D.C.: TESOL.

Mohan, B. A. 1979(c). "Language Teaching and Content Teaching." *TESOL Quarterly* 13(2): 171–182.

Mohan, B. A. 1982. "Language, Content and the Interactive Principle." *TEAL '81/TESL Canada Conference Proceedings 1981*: 11–16.

Mohan, B. A., and N. Katz. 1977. "Communicative Competence and Flowcharts." *TESL Talk* 8(1):25–31.

Mollica, A. 1976. "Cartoons in the Language Classroom." *Canadian Modern Language Review* 32–34:424–44.

Moore, P., and H. Thomas. 1976. *The Anatomy of Decisions*. Harmondsworth, Middlesex: Penguin Books.

Nelson, G. and T. Winters. 1980. *ESL Operations: Techniques for Learning While Doing*. Rowley, Mass.: Newbury House.

Newport, E., H. Gleitman and L. Gleitman. 1977. "Mother, I'd Rather Do it Myself: Some Effects and Non-effects of Maternal Speech Style." In C. Snow and C. Ferguson (eds) *Talking to Children*, 100–149. New York: Cambridge University Press.

Oller, J., and K. Perkins. 1978. *Language in Education: Testing the Tests*. Rowley, Mass.: Newbury House.

Oller, J. 1979. *Language Tests at School*. London: Longman.

Ore, O. 1963. *Graphs and Their Uses*. New York: Random House.

Paulston, C. 1980. *Bilingual Education: Theories and Issues*. Rowley, Mass: Newbury House.

Pearn, M. 1978. *Employment Testing and the Goal of Equal Opportunity: The American Experience*. London: The Runnymede Trust.

Peters, R. S. 1966. *Ethics and Education*. London: Allen and Unwin.

Prabhu, N. 1983. *Procedural Syllabuses*. Singapore: SEAMEO Regional Language Centre, 18th Regional Seminar.

Priestly, P., et al. 1978. *Social Skills and Personal Problem Solving*. London: Tavistock Publications.

Reitburger, R., and W. Fuchs. 1972. *Comics: Anatomy of a Mass Medium*. Boston: Little Brown.

Rescher, N. 1969. *Introduction to Value Theory*. Englewood Cliffs, N.J.: Prentice-Hall.

Reynolds, C. R., and T. Gutkin (eds). 1982. *The Handbook of School Psychology*. New York: John Wiley.

Robinson, P. 1980. *ESP: English for Specific Purposes*. Oxford: Pergamon Press.

Russell, B. 1912. *The Problems of Philosophy*. London: Oxford University Press.

Sampson, G. 1977. "A Real Challenge to ESL Methodology." *TESOL Quarterly* 11(3):241–256.

Saville-Troike, M. 1976. *Foundations for Teaching English as a Second Language*. Englewood Cliffs, N.J.: Prentice-Hall.

Seelye, H. 1974. *Teaching Culture: Strategies for Foreign Language Educators*. Skokie, Ill.: National Textbook Co.

Shorthouse, A., et al. 1980. *English Through Nutrition*. Vancouver, B.C.: Vancouver School Board.

Singer, H., and D. Donlan. 1980. *Reading and Learning from Text*. Boston: Little, Brown.

Skyrms, B. 1966. *Choice and Chance: An Introduction to Inductive Logic*. Belmont, California: Dickenson Publishing Co.

Stern, H. 1983. *Fundamental Concepts of Language Teaching*. Oxford: Oxford University Press.

Stoddart, J., and F. Stoddart. 1968. *The Teaching of English to Immigrant Children*. London: University of London Press.

Strawson, P. F. 1959. *Individuals*. London: Methuen.

Stubbs, M. 1980. *Language and Literacy: the Sociolinguistics of Reading and Writing*. London: Routledge and Kegan Paul.

Swain, M. 1974. "French Immersion Programs Across Canada: Research Findings." *Canadian Modern Language Review* 31(2): 117–129.

Swain, M., and S. Lapkin. 1982. *Evaluating Bilingual Education: A Canadian Case Study*. Clevedon, Avon: Multilingual Matters.

Tucker, R., and A. D'Anglejan. 1975. "New Directions in Second Language Teaching." In R. C. Troike and N. Modiano (eds) *Proceeding of the First Inter-American Conference on Bilingual Education*, 63–72. Arlington, Va.: Center for Applied Linguistics.

Twining, W., and D. Miers. 1976. *How to Do Things with Rules*. London: Weidenfield and Nicholson.

Urzua, C. 1981. *Talking Purposefully*. Silver Springs, Maryland: Institute of Modern Languages.

Von Wright, G. 1960. *A Treatise on Induction and Probability*. Patterson, N.J.: Littlefield, Adams and Co.

Von Wright, G. 1971. *Explanation and Understanding*. Ithaca, N.Y.: Cornell University Press.

Wakefield, P., et al. 1981. *English as a Second Language/Dialect Resource Book for K-12*. Victoria, B.C.: Ministry of Education.

Wallerstein, N. 1983. *Language and Culture in Conflict*. Reading, Mass.: Addison-Wesley.

Wheatley, D., and A. Unwin. 1972. *The Algorithm Writer's Guide*. London: Longman.

Whitman, M. 1981. *Writing: the Nature, Development and Teaching of Written Communication*. vol. 1. Hillsdale, N.J.: Erlbaum.

Whitney, N., et al. 1980. *Language Across the Curriculum: Progress Report*. London: Ealing College of Higher Education.

Whitney, N. 1982. "The ESL Teacher as a Good Colleague." *TEAL '81/TESL Canada Conference Proceedings 1981*: 17–22.

Widdowson, H. 1978. *Teaching Language as Communication*. Oxford: Oxford University Press.

Widdowson, H. (ed.) 1979. *Reading and Thinking in English*. Oxford: Oxford University Press.

Wilkins, D. A. 1976. *Notional Syllabuses*. London: Oxford University Press.

Williams, J. 1977. *Learning to Write, or Writing to Learn?*. Slough: National Foundation for Educational Research.

Willis, J. 1982. *Teaching English through English*. London: Longman.

Wright, A. 1976. *Visual Materials for the Language Teacher*. London: Longman.

Yorkey, R. 1970. *Study Skills for Students of English as a Second Language*. New York: McGraw-Hill.